Quick

ANSWERS

for Busy Teachers

Quick ANSWERS for *Busy* Teachers

Solutions to 60 Common Challenges

Annette Breaux | Todd Whitaker

JB JOSSEY-BASS™

A Wiley Brand

Cover Design: Wiley

Cover Art: © VikaSuh | Shutterstock

Published by Jossey-Bass

A Wiley Brand

One Montgomery Street, Suite 1200, San Francisco, CA 94104-4594—www.josseybass.com

Jossey-Bass books and products are available through most bookstores. To contact Jossey-Bass directly call our Customer Care Department within the U.S. at 800-956-7739, outside the U.S. at 317-572-3986, or fax 317-572-4002.

Wiley publishes in a variety of print and electronic formats and by print-on-demand. Some material included with standard print versions of this book may not be included in e-books or in print-on-demand. If this book refers to media such as a CD or DVD that is not included in the version you purchased, you may download this material at http://booksupport.wiley.com. For more information about Wiley products, visit www.wiley.com.

Library of Congress Cataloging-in-Publication Data is on file.

ISBN 978-1-118-92062-6 (pbk.)
ISBN 978-1-118-92063-3 (ebk.)
ISBN 978-1-118-92064-0 (ebk.)

Printed in the United States of America

FIRST EDITION

PB Printing   10 9 8 7 6 5 4 3 2 1

CONTENTS

■ ■ ■

■ ■ ■

ABOUT THE AUTHORS

Annette Breaux is one of the most entertaining and informative authors and speakers in education today. She leaves her audiences with practical techniques to implement in their classrooms immediately. Administrators agree that they see results from teachers the next day.

Annette is a former classroom teacher, curriculum coordinator, and author of Louisiana FIRST, a statewide induction program for new teachers. Annette also served as the teacher induction coordinator for Nicholls State University in Thibodaux, Louisiana. She coauthored a book with Dr. Harry K. Wong on new teacher induction.

Her other writings include *101 Answers for New Teachers and Their Mentors; Real Teachers, Real Challenges, Real Solutions; 101 Poems for Teachers; Seven Simple Secrets: What the Best Teachers Know and Do; 50 Ways to Improve Student Behavior; Making Good Teaching Great;* and *The Ten-Minute Inservice.*

Teachers who have read Annette's writings or heard her speak agree that they come away with user-friendly information, heartfelt inspiration, and a much-needed reminder that theirs is the most noble of all professions.

Dr. Todd Whitaker has been fortunate to be able to blend his passion with his career. He is recognized as a leading presenter in the field of education, and his message about the importance of teaching has resonated with hundreds of thousands of educators around the world. Todd is a professor of educational leadership at Indiana State University in Terre Haute, Indiana, and he has spent his life pursuing his love of education by researching and studying effective teachers and principals.

Prior to moving into higher education, Todd was a math teacher and basketball coach in Missouri. He then served as a principal at the middle school, junior high, and high school levels. He was also a middle school coordinator in charge of staffing, curriculum, and technology for the opening of new middle schools.

One of the nation's leading authorities on staff motivation, teacher leadership, and principal effectiveness, Todd has written thirty books, including the national best seller *What Great Teachers Do Differently*. Other titles include *Shifting the Monkey; Dealing with Difficult Teachers; Teaching Matters; Great Quotes for Great Educators; What Great Principals Do Differently; Motivating and Inspiring Teachers;* and *Dealing with Difficult Parents*.

Todd is married to Beth, also a former teacher and principal, who is a professor of elementary education at Indiana State University. They are the parents of three children: Katherine, Madeline, and Harrison.

PREFACE

D o you remember your first year of teaching? When you couldn't wait until your second year because surely you would be less busy? When you would have all of your lesson plans from the previous year already completed, ready to be implemented? When you would have this "teaching thing" mastered? It doesn't take any teacher very long to realize that teaching is time-consuming, no matter how many years you've been doing it. A teacher who's not busy is a teacher who's not effective! But please don't take that to mean that all busy teachers are effective teachers. They're not. In fact, some of the most effective teachers are not nearly as busy as their less effective coworkers. Effective teachers do work hard, of course, but they don't have to put in as many hours as some of their less effective counterparts. And they're not nearly as stressed.

These teachers often appear to lead a charmed life. They seem to get the "good" students every year . They walk the halls smiling. The administrators like them. The parents like them. And everything just seems to fall into place for them. The truth is that they do sort of lead a charmed life—at least at school. They're simply implementing basic techniques that less effective teachers don't yet know about. If that sounds overly simplified, it's not.

As educators, authors, and consultants, we have made it our lives' work to study the secrets of successful teachers. And it continues to be our privilege to share these secrets with teachers worldwide. We've learned that *all* teachers want to be better. We've learned that teachers are some of the most genuinely "good" people on the planet. We've learned that all teachers face common classroom challenges. But the best teachers handle these challenges much differently from all the rest—thus, their "charmed lives."

This book will address common challenges that many teachers face on a daily basis, regardless of grade level or subject area taught. The tips, suggestions, and answers within the book come from studying what separates the best from the rest. Nothing in the book is difficult or time-consuming. (In fact, you might learn that what you're currently doing is much more difficult and time-consuming than it needs to be.) Reading it should help you reevaluate how you typically deal with common challenges at school. Implementing the strategies will help to increase your effectiveness as a teacher. Do you want to see increased student achievement and better student behavior, while experiencing more joy in teaching and less stress in your job? Then learn just what it is that the most successful teachers do.

We are highly aware that no two teachers are exactly alike and that no one solution fits all circumstances. Instead, our goal is to provide ideas and strategies for you to use exactly when you need them. Depending on your situation or career point, some of these may be revolutionary, while others may help provide a simple tweak or a friendly reminder. Oftentimes, due to your demanding and busy life, you may find yourself drifting away from past practices that had a positive impact on your students. Thus we have attempted to provide time-efficient ideas, tips, and strategies that apply to the most common challenges educators face. What you do as a teacher is tremendously important. With this book we hope to support the essential role you play in the lives of students.

HOW TO USE THIS BOOK

Though this book can certainly be read cover to cover, it can also be read in no particular order. You might want to select topics from the Contents that address your immediate needs and read those sections first. If you're a *teacher* who does not struggle with classroom management issues, skip that part for now. But do come back to it later, because you might find a few new ideas to help you become even more effective in that area.

If you're a *mentor*, you might choose to use this book for ideas to help a new teacher you are mentoring deal more effectively with certain challenges he or she is facing.

Each of the book's topics can serve as stand-alone inservice material for *administrators* or *staff development trainers* to use at faculty meetings. Administrators may also choose to use ideas in the book for suggestions to share with individual teachers in need of assistance.

The book addresses sixty common challenges that most teachers face. It is written in a simple, easy-to-follow format. Each section is divided into three parts:

1. *If This Happens*, where the challenge is discussed

2. *Try This*, where suggestions for meeting and overcoming the challenge are provided

3. *Remember*, where a summary and a few reminders are provided for each challenge

Though we do not suggest that this book addresses every challenge teachers will ever face, we have attempted to include those that are most common to most educators. Each challenge is addressed in a straightforward, no-frills manner, providing quick, simple tips and suggestions for overcoming each.

These tips and suggestions come straight from the classrooms of highly effective teachers.

Note that many sections in this book include material that can be displayed during a presentation or handed out to teachers during inservices. Those materials are available for free download from our publisher's website, at www.wiley.com/go/quickanswers, using the password 20626. Throughout the book, we'll remind you which materials can be downloaded by displaying the following icon:

Quick

ANSWERS

for **Busy Teachers**

*We dedicate this
book to the memory of
Amy Simon Breaux—
Annette's mother,
Todd's biggest fan, and
devoted teacher.*

PART ONE

Challenges with Students

1

THE CLASS CLOWN IS NOT HUMORING YOU

IF THIS HAPPENS

There's one in every class. He's known, not always affectionately, as the class clown. He loves the limelight and he seeks it out at all costs. He takes any situation, even serious ones, and tries to insinuate his humor. Though his antics can be annoying, he's often clever, and his jokes are sometimes funny. You can't dispute his creativity. He has a loyal following, his very own "groupies" who love to egg him on. Other students roll their eyes, finding him a nuisance. When he's in your classroom you often find yourself on edge, trying to anticipate his next wisecrack and prepare for how you'll handle it.

The bottom line is that the class clown is seeking attention. And he's getting it. (Research has shown that the vast majority of student misbehavior stems from attention seeking.) You, as the professional in the classroom, realize that there's a reason this student is craving attention. Maybe he is struggling with issues at home; maybe he's struggling with issues at school; and almost always he lacks maturity and/or self-respect.

So what can you do? First, realize that the class clown is not out to get you, so take care not to take his antics personally. Rather, he's attempting to feel important and to get attention. Knowing this will help you deal with the situation more mindfully and effectively, and less emotionally.

TRY THIS

The following are several ways to deal appropriately with a class clown:

- Occasionally, when it is appropriate, it's okay to laugh when the class clown says something funny. You never want to send the message that humor is not acceptable in your classroom. On the contrary, humor is an important part of any classroom—appropriate humor, that is.

- Make sure that you discuss with your entire class the difference between appropriate and inappropriate humor. Tell them that there is a time for work and a time for play. Give examples of appropriate and inappropriate humor.

- Be careful never to appear angry with or personally offended by the class clown. This will only serve to worsen an already tenuous situation. It will tell him that he is controlling your emotions, and that's the last message you want to send. No one repeats a behavior unless he's receiving some kind of "reward" for that behavior. Sometimes that reward is inadvertently coming from the teacher.

- Speak with the class clown privately. Explain that you appreciate his intellect, his creativity, and his quick wit. Add, however, that sometimes his humor is not appropriate. Give him specific examples of when his humor has been both appropriate and inappropriate. Tell him that you would like to help him act in a more responsible and mature way. Express your concern about the idea that something is bothering him and offer the opportunity for him to share what's bothering him. (Don't be surprised, however, if he denies that anything is bothering him. Don't push. Just let him know that you care and that you are always available if he needs to talk to someone.)

- Establish some kind of signal with the class clown. When his humor is inappropriate, simply use the signal to let him know that the behavior needs to stop. Try to make the signal as subtle as possible.

- Begin giving the class clown more and more positive attention when he is *not* clowning around. As often as possible, recognize any evidence of appropriate behavior on his part and comment on it.

- When you begin to notice a turnaround, small as it may be, speak with the class clown privately and say, "I've noticed you're really making an effort to use your humor more appropriately. That takes maturity, and I'm proud of you. Keep up the good work!"

Using these techniques almost always yields immediate and positive results.

DON'T FORGET

- A class clown is seeking attention—and always for a reason. If possible, try to determine the reason.
- Never take the class clown's inappropriate behavior personally.
- Laughter is a good thing—when it is appropriate. Make sure your students know this, and make sure that you share your humorous side with them also.
- Teach the class clown the difference between appropriate and inappropriate humor. Help him to use his humor more appropriately.
- Give the class clown positive attention when he is not clowning around.
- Be patient. Bad habits are never broken overnight.

2

A STUDENT IS REFUSING TO DO WORK

IF THIS HAPPENS

We've all been there. You give an assignment and everyone gets busy on the assignment. Everyone, that is, but one student. This has become a pattern with the student. You've reached a point where you can predict, before you give the assignment, that she will either put her head down or look around as if to say, "Why are you all bothering to do this? I'm not doing this. This is stupid." On occasion, she has actually gone beyond thinking those thoughts and verbalized them. You've tried telling her to get busy, and she ignores you. You've resorted to threatening her. "If you don't get busy, then . . . ," and you promise some type of consequence. Her attitude is "I don't care what you say or do. I'm not doing this assignment." You may even have resorted to sending her to the principal's office. Each time, you've gotten upset about the situation. And the student knows that. You don't want to engage in yet another power struggle with this student, but you don't know what else to do. Her grades are suffering, but it doesn't seem to bother her.

TRY THIS

First, understand that when a student is refusing to do her work, there is always a reason. And before you can solve the problem, you have to identify what's causing it.

Here are a few of the most common reasons that students refuse to do their work:

- The student is dealing with a personal problem either at home or at school.

- The student is seeking attention from her peers.

- The student is trying to control you. (Sometimes behavior problems stem from a student's need for power.)

- The student is afraid to fail, so she's taking control of that failure. In other words, "It's better not to try and be in control of the failure than to give it my best and fail because I just can't do the work."

Your first priority is to uncover the reason behind the behavior. Then you'll be better equipped to solve the problem.

A teacher was speaking about a problem with a student who was refusing to do her work. "She hardly does anything in class. And the sad fact is that she's capable. She could make As if she wanted to. But she won't apply herself." We asked the teacher what she thought the reason was behind the behavior. "I have no idea," she said. "I think she's just lazy." We then asked the teacher if the student knew that she cared about her. She answered, "How can *I* care about a student who doesn't care about herself?" Aha! We had an answer. You see, this teacher was taking the student's behavior personally. She was angry with her for not doing her work. Though she didn't realize it, her actions toward this student were speaking volumes. And the student was picking up on this. The student was determined to "get her," even if it meant failing. If this student felt that her teacher didn't care about her, she was right.

We spoke with another teacher facing a very similar problem. She was a teacher who definitely cared about her students—all of them. She said, "I couldn't figure out what was going on with one of my students. He suddenly wouldn't do any work in class. He just sat there and sulked. When I asked him to get busy, he said he wasn't going to do his work because he didn't care about it. I was worried about him and I was determined to help him. I pulled him aside and told him as much. I told him I really wanted to help him, but he had to help me to understand what was going on first. He burst into tears and told me that his father had recently been sent to prison. I wanted to cry. Instead, I told him I was here for him, no matter what. If he wanted to talk, I would listen. If he wanted to cry, his tears were safe with me. I told him if he needed extra help at recess, I would give my own time to sit and help him. He was so appreciative of my caring and understanding that he immediately began doing all of his work in class. And I was sure to give him special attention and a warm smile every day. I didn't solve his problems at home, but I did provide a safe, welcoming environment at school where he could feel loved and successful."

There's always a reason when a student is refusing to do his work. Always. And your job is to try to determine that reason and then help the student to overcome whatever problems he is facing. If he doesn't understand the material, provide some remediation. If he is having a problem and is willing to discuss it, listen. If he's trying to engage you in a power struggle, don't participate. As the saying goes, "You can attract more bees with honey than with vinegar." Approach the student with compassion and calmly ask, "Would you like some help getting started on your work?" And then do just that—help him. But at all costs, avoid appearing angry or frustrated with the student, because that approach is never successful.

DON'T FORGET

- When a student is refusing to do his work, try to determine the reason first.

- If a student is overwhelmed with material he does not understand, provide remediation.

- If a student is struggling with a problem at home (or at school) and wants to talk about it, then listen. There will be times when the problem requires the help of a parent, an administrator, or a school counselor. Seek that help if necessary.

- Make every effort to ensure that the student knows you care about him and are willing to help.

- Don't ever allow yourself to engage in a struggle for power with a student. You'll lose every time. Instead, talk to the student calmly and offer to help. Act out of concern, not frustration.

- Remember that students work harder and behave better with teachers who care about them. Express your caring and concern on a daily basis.

3

SEVERAL STUDENTS DISLIKE YOU

IF THIS HAPPENS

As teachers, we walk a fine line. We're the adults in the classroom, charged with educating students, none of whom are adults. We wear many hats— teacher, nurse, role model, decision maker, motivational speaker, listener, coach, cheerleader, sympathizer, authority figure, enforcer of rules, confidant, counselor, conveyer of knowledge, and so on. But are we our students' friend? While it's true that we should act friendly toward our students (as opposed to unfriendly), we should not attempt to be their buddy or their pal. Students will lose respect quickly for teachers who attempt to act as their friends would act, to be one of them, so to speak. We're *not* one of them. And if they ever view us as "one of them," our influence will be lessened.

Does it matter if your students like you or not? Yes, it does. Think of a few people you do not like. Would you enjoy being in a classroom every day with them? Would you be inclined to listen to them, respect them, and learn from them? Not likely. It is important that our students like us, because then they will be more likely to learn from us. If a student doesn't like you, she may go beyond simply not learning from you and become a behavior problem.

When a student dislikes a teacher, she is likely to display one or more of the following behaviors:

- Act withdrawn
- Give the teacher angry looks
- Attempt to counteract whatever the teacher says or does
- Say hurtful things to the teacher
- Refuse to work
- Refuse to pay attention
- Speak ill of the teacher to others
- Display a bad attitude toward the teacher and possibly others in the classroom

So when a student displays any of these behaviors, does it always stem from a dislike of the teacher? No. Sometimes a student is faced with problems at home or elsewhere, and she acts withdrawn or angry at school. This is not a reflection on the teacher. When a student does not pay attention in class, there are numerous possible reasons for that behavior. However, it is usually fairly easy to determine if a student likes you or not. There's a difference between acting badly in the presence of someone and acting badly *toward* someone.

TRY THIS

So what do you do if you have one or more students who you know do not like you?

First, try to determine why it is that the student dislikes you. We would caution against simply asking, "Hey, why don't you like me?" That will only serve to make the student feel powerful over you. She may think, "Good, she noticed. And it's bothering her." That's a powerful feeling for a student, to know she is controlling an adult's emotions. Instead, look back at when the student's unfriendly actions began. Maybe she misbehaved and you punished her. (You were not wrong to punish a misbehaving student, by the way, so we're definitely not suggesting that you should not hold students accountable.) You may realize that you could have handled the situation differently. Or you may feel good about how you handled the situation. But at least you know where the pattern started. You might want to take the student aside and ask, "Is something bothering you? You're not acting like yourself, and that worries me. Can I do anything to help?" This way, you're letting the student know that you care and are concerned, but you're not implying that her actions are affecting you personally.

Sometimes the problem is that the student does not think that you like her or care about her. That's an easy fix. Begin immediately to make a special effort to let her know that you like her. You like her a lot! (See Topic 15: Some Students Are Easier to Like Than Others.)

If you determine that several students don't like you, take a close look at what it is you might be doing to foster that dislike. And begin to work immediately at turning that around.

DON'T FORGET

If you determine that one or more students do not like you, consider the following:

- Students learn best from teachers they like and trust.
- Students like teachers who they feel like and trust them.
- Though you do not want to be viewed as a student's friend or buddy, it is important that you act friendly toward all of your students.
- Once you have determined why a student does not like you, you can immediately begin to work on repairing the relationship.

4

YOU EMBARRASSED A STUDENT IN FRONT OF HIS PEERS

IF THIS HAPPENS

You were having a bad day. You woke up not feeling well, but you came to work anyway. All you could think about was making it through the day. You announced to your students that you were not feeling well, hoping they would be kind enough to behave their best. During second period, you collected the homework assignments. Yet again, James did not have his assignment. Before he could explain, you lashed out. You told him in front of the rest of the class that you were tired of his excuses and tired of his irresponsibility. You dared him to miss another assignment. Your voice was elevated, your face was tense, and your gestures were intimidating. James put his head down. You thought you saw him quickly wipe a tear from his eye, but his head was down, so you couldn't be sure. Regardless, you wanted to take back what you had just said to him. To make matters worse, one of the other students said, "James was at the hospital all night. His grandfather had a heart attack, and they don't know if he's going to make it."

You wanted the earth to swallow you. You felt awful for James, and you were appalled by your recent actions. And you thought *you* were having a bad day? Suddenly, your stuffy head wasn't such a big deal after all. A student in your care was hurting, and you had just poured salt into an open wound. And now you had to figure out how to handle a delicate situation appropriately.

It has happened to many of us. Intentionally or not, we have acted unprofessionally with a student, embarrassing him in front of his peers. When we realize what we've done, we're faced with trying to repair the damage in the most appropriate way possible.

TRY THIS

If you've embarrassed a student in front of his peers, there is one thing you should do: apologize. The apology should be offered in front of everyone, not privately with the student. You see, the embarrassment was partly due to the fact that the misfortunate incident occurred in front of an audience. So the same audience should witness the apology.

What does an appropriate apology look and sound like?

- First, be careful to resist the temptation to justify your actions in any way. For example, don't say, "I'm sorry about your grandfather, and I'm sorry I lost my temper with you, but you have a history of not turning in homework, so you can understand why I might have assumed you just didn't do your assignment yet again." This is not a genuine apology, and it will only serve to further damage your relationship with the student.

- Look at the student and genuinely apologize. Don't just say you're sorry. Tell him exactly why you are sorry for your actions. Say, "James, I'm very sorry I lost my temper with you. That was wrong of me, and you did not deserve to be treated that way. I know I've hurt you, and I apologize for my actions." If you're tempted to explain that you're not feeling well today, resist that temptation. Feeling lousy does not give us license to make others feel lousy too.

- Ask for forgiveness. Say, "I hope you can forgive me. I'll do my best never to do that again." Following the apology, tell him privately that you are very sorry to hear about his grandfather. Let him know he can come to you if he needs someone to talk to.

You've restored the student's dignity, you've hopefully been able to repair the relationship, and you've demonstrated (for James and his classmates) how to apologize appropriately. Lesson learned for you, and lesson taught to the students. Without realizing it, you may also have repaired your relationship with the class. Students don't like to see their peers humiliated.

All that's left to do is to work hard at proving to James and the class that you learn from your mistakes and do not repeat them. By the way, would your actions have been appropriate if James had simply not turned in his homework again? No. It is never appropriate to humiliate a student, privately or publicly. If he had failed to turn in his homework with no reasonable excuse, it would have been appropriate to speak with him privately and possibly attach a consequence to his actions. It might have sounded like this: "James, I'm disappointed that you haven't turned in your homework again, and as we discussed, there's going to be a consequence this time." Decide on a logical consequence, and then wipe the slate clean. The next time you assign homework, encourage James to remember to do his assignment. Say, "I'm counting on you to do your homework. Thanks."

DON'T FORGET

When an apology is heartfelt and genuine, a student will almost always forgive you. And when you apologize in front of the class, you help to restore the student's dignity. You also serve as a role model for all the students of how to admit your mistakes and offer a sincere apology for your actions.

5

STUDENTS WHO DON'T BEHAVE IN YOUR CLASS ARE BEHAVING FOR ANOTHER TEACHER

IF THIS HAPPENS

Why is it that some children behave differently with one parent than they do with another? Or that some students behave differently at home than they do at school? Or that some students behave differently with different teachers? The answer is simple: students behave differently in different environments. They quickly learn, in each environment, what the expectations, rules, and procedures are. They know what's acceptable to some and unacceptable to others. They know whose buttons they can and can't push. They know, in each environment, what they can and cannot get away with.

Marvin was a first-year teacher who, like many new teachers, was struggling with classroom management. The students had gotten completely out of hand—talking, running around, bothering others, sleeping, laughing, and doing very little, if any, schoolwork in his class. He begged and pleaded, he flicked the lights on and off, he threatened them, he yelled at them, he sent many to the principal, he held parent conferences, and he tried everything he knew to get the students to pay attention—all to no avail. The situation was spiraling out of control, and so was Marvin.

Denise, a master teacher, was assigned to help Marvin try to turn things around. During the conference following Denise's first observation of Marvin, he told her it really wasn't his fault. These students were spoiled and lazy, and they wouldn't respond to anything he said or did. Denise decided to take Marvin to observe his students in the classroom of Mike, another teacher who taught the same students. Mike had several years of experience under his belt and was a master at classroom management. He loved teaching, he appeared to love every student, and the students loved him right back. After observing in Mike's classroom, Marvin turned to Denise and said, "I think that maybe my behavior is affecting theirs. I notice that the students behave differently for Mike, but I also realize that Mike behaves differently than I do. So if I change my behavior, maybe the students' behavior will change too!" Denise explained to Marvin that it wasn't "him," but rather it was his lack of management skills coupled with his less-than-positive attitude toward the students. Denise and Marvin continued to observe Mike, taking note of everything he did to manage his classroom. Then Denise helped Marvin do those same things in his own classroom. Within a day, there was a noted difference, but within a few weeks, the turnaround was phenomenal. For the rest of the year, Marvin continued to seek the advice and counsel of other successful teachers. All of these teachers were happy to help and honored to be asked for their assistance. Today, Marvin is a master teacher who helps other teachers who struggle with management issues.

Do you have any students who do not behave well with you, but are behaving well with a fellow teacher? Maybe your situation is not as chaotic as Marvin's, but, left unattended, it could get that way.

TRY THIS

Following are the management strategies Marvin learned from observing Mike:

- Establish a simple, clear set of rules and procedures.
- Have a discussion with the students, explaining the new rules and procedures.

- Establish a way for getting the attention of your students. (See Topic 28: Students Enter Your Class and Immediately Begin Talking.)

- Maintain a calm voice and a professional demeanor, regardless of the students' behavior. If you do what Marvin did and allow the students to see your frustrations, things will quickly go from bad to worse.

- Remain consistent with your rules and procedures. Hold students accountable for their actions, but do so calmly and professionally.

- Smile often and appear to love teaching every minute of every day.

- Take a special interest in all of your students, especially those who are the most challenging.

DON'T FORGET

If students who don't behave well with you are behaving well with another teacher, don't be too proud to ask that teacher for her secrets. Observe that student (or students) in this teacher's classroom if possible. Discuss with this teacher her management plan. Ask for particular strategies she uses with the students.

At one time or another, we all learn from each other. Don't fall into the trap of thinking, "If I ask for her help, she'll think I'm an ineffective teacher." None of us know all the answers. But if you let your pride stand in the way of asking for help, you're doing a disservice to yourself and your students.

On an added note, resist the temptation to seek teachers who are having the very same problems you are. You may be able to commiserate, and you might both feel better for a while, but you won't be helping yourselves or the students in the long run. Instead, encourage that teacher to come along as you seek advice from teachers who are *not* having the same problems. Then both of you can work at becoming more effective together.

6

YOU'RE NOT SURE IF A BEHAVIOR CONSEQUENCE WAS APPROPRIATE

IF THIS HAPPENS

Scenario 1

Margo had a strict policy in her classroom regarding cell phones. They had to be off during class. No texting was allowed at any time. One day, as the students were busy with an assignment, she noticed that Jamal had his cell phone out and was obviously texting. She walked up to his desk and took his phone. Her suspicions were confirmed. "Jamal, what is the policy about cell phones?" she asked. "No texting," he replied. She said, "Well, since you didn't follow the policy, I want you to send a text to your mother and tell her that you did not follow the policy and were caught texting in my class." Jamal sent the text.

Think about what just happened. A teacher had a no-texting policy. A student did not follow the policy and sent a text. As part of his punishment, he was required to send another text. Isn't there a mixed message here? Clearly, the teacher had not thought this one through. What would have been a more appropriate consequence? A more appropriate consequence may have been for Margo to hold Jamal's phone for him until the end of class.

Scenario 2

In another classroom, Kate had a policy stating that using personal social media sites was not allowed during class time. On this particular day, Maria and Gina were at their computer station reading posts of friends on their favorite social media site. (They were supposed to be doing on-line research for a current class project.) Kate walked up to them and whispered, "I know you know you're supposed to be working on your project. It seems you forgot the rule about not accessing social media sites during class time." The girls apologized. Kate said, "Why don't you just go back to your desks and work on the writing phase of the project for now? Maybe we'll give the computer station another try tomorrow." Everyone else continued to work at their computer stations for the remainder of the activity. Maria and Gina worked alone at their desks.

Think about what just happened. There was a specific policy regarding the use of social media during class time. Two students did not follow the policy, so there was a logical consequence. No drama. No power struggle. They didn't use the computer station appropriately, so they were not allowed to use the computer station for the rest of the class period.

Scenario 3

Pat was allowing her students to work together in groups. Before she did this, there had been a class discussion about the importance of students getting along with each other within the groups and keeping the noise down to whispers. During the group activity, several group members began complaining that John was making aggravating noises. Pat had heard the noises and was trying to determine who had been making them. She took John aside and said, "Go sit out in the hall and make all the noises you want." She left him there until the end of the group activity.

Consider what happened. There was an assignment given. The students were allowed to work on the assignment in groups. John displayed an unwillingness to work cooperatively with his group. The teacher then put him in the hall and allowed him to continue the misbehavior. So the noise problem was eliminated inside the classroom. True. But he was simply allowed to continue making the noises elsewhere, and this time he didn't even have to do his schoolwork. Not a bad deal in the student's mind! Consider this: we have a student who is not behaving when we are looking—and our answer to this is to put him out in the hallway, hoping he behaves when we are *not* looking.

A more appropriate consequence might have been to first speak with John and say, "You're disturbing the group with your noises. If you continue to do that, you won't be able to work with the group. You decide." If the behavior continued, she could then remove John from the group and have him work on his own. That would have been much more logical and more beneficial to the student.

TRY THIS

As teachers, we often second-guess ourselves. We want to do what's right and fair and best for our students. So when a student's actions warrant a consequence, how can you be sure that the consequence is an appropriate one?

- Remember first that every little misbehavior does not necessarily warrant a consequence. Sometimes, if the infraction is minor, it can be ignored. For instance, if a student whispers something to another student one time, it can usually be ignored. Consequences are typically reserved for more serious offenses. In the case of John making noises in the group, his actions were distracting to the rest of the group, so it was logical to remove him from the group.

- If you determine that a behavior warrants a consequence, make sure that the consequence is a logical one and that it fits the misbehavior.

- Be careful to attack the problem and not the person. Don't let your emotions get involved when a student misbehaves. Tell the student about the consequence in a calm voice. You can be serious and matter-of-fact without appearing angry or mean. You can help the student to realize he is in control of his choices by saying things like, "You can either do your work now or at recess. It's up to you."

- Following a behavior infraction, always talk to the student and discuss a more appropriate way for him to respond to a similar situation in the future. Don't ever assume that just because a student suffered a consequence, he now knows how to make a more responsible choice in the future.

DON'T FORGET

It's important that students learn to be respectful and responsible. In the classrooms of effective teachers, students quickly learn that negative choices have negative consequences. And in order for those consequences to be effective—causing the student to think twice before acting that way again and realizing why what he did was inappropriate—they have to be logical. If a student calls another student an ugly name, it is not logical to keep him in at recess for several days. A more logical approach is to talk to him about what he did, help him to see that his actions hurt another, and then have him apologize to the student whose feelings he hurt. Consequences are most effective when they are logical, when they are relevant (meaning that the consequence relates to the actual behavior), and when students understand *why* their actions were irresponsible and *how* they can make more responsible choices next time.

7

YOU'RE UNSURE WHEN TO REFER A STUDENT TO THE OFFICE

IF THIS HAPPENS

The age-old question continues to be asked: "Should teachers send students to the principal's office for discipline infractions?" There's no simple yes-or-no answer. More easily answered questions would be: "What types of behaviors warrant discipline referrals?" and "What message does it send to students when a teacher often sends students to the principal for misbehavior?" (The key word in the latter question is *often.*) Speaking of *often,* it is often said (and most principals will readily agree) that more than 90 percent of discipline referrals come from about 10 percent of all teachers. Any principal can readily predict today who will send the most students to the office tomorrow.

So what message does it send when a teacher frequently sends students to the office for minor behavior infractions? The message is that the teacher is not really in charge. Someone else (in an office away from the classroom) is in charge. Though that is never the message the teacher wants to convey, it is always the message the students receive.

Consider this example. A teacher who relies too heavily on the principal to manage her discipline challenges sends yet another student to the office because she's tired of his talking in class. The student goes to the office, but he soon returns, with a smile on his face. And then the very predictable question is asked, "What happened?" The student almost always gives the same response: "Nothing." And now the teacher is even more upset than when she sent the student to the office. She has forgotten that all students say that nothing happened. It doesn't actually mean that nothing happened; it means that the student is saving face. If she really wants an accurate answer, she's going to have to ask the principal. But usually, if the teacher questions the principal and the principal says, "We had a good talk and discussed how he should handle himself differently next time," the teacher is upset by this. "What? That's it? They talked?" complains the teacher to one or more co-workers. "A lot of good that's going to do. No wonder the students behave so badly in my classroom!" So what is it that this teacher thinks the principal should do in the *office* that will cause the student to behave differently in her *classroom*? Remember—we're not dealing with serious offenses in this scenario. We're talking about minor infractions that are destined to increase in frequency if the teacher does not establish some control. Though sometimes the principal can serve to put a Band-Aid on the situation, the remedy will be temporary at best, as long as the teacher continues to lack classroom management skills. Perhaps a question all teachers need to ask themselves might be, "Is it ever appropriate to ask a student what happened when he returns from the office?" Most likely the answer is no.

So is it ever appropriate to send a student to the principal for discipline problems? Yes, when the situation is serious. Let's say that a student gets violent. Most principals usually insist that teachers refer students for violent behavior. But those situations are the exception, not the rule. The teachers representing the 10 percent mentioned earlier are rarely sending students to the office for serious offenses. Most of their referrals are for minor aggravations that could and should be handled in the classroom. If, however, one of the 90 percent who almost never sends students to the office sends a student to the principal, the principal takes it seriously. And so does the student.

TRY THIS

If you're unsure about when it is or is not appropriate and/or necessary to send students to the office, simply ask. Ask your principal what kinds of situations she feels should require that a student be sent to the office and which should be handled by the teachers. A general rule is that anything that *can* be handled in the classroom *should* be handled in the classroom.

Remember that there are, however, serious behavior offenses that require sending a student to the office. Determine which behaviors warrant an office referral, and be sure the students are made aware of these. If the school has a rule stating that any violent behavior results in an office referral, then the students should be made aware of this. If a student brings a banned substance into the classroom, it's a no-brainer that the office will want to deal with this. But when serious offenses occur, students already know that the office insists on dealing with the issue, so it doesn't lessen the teacher's authority in their minds. In essence, the student chose a behavior knowing it was a serious offense, so the student actually sent himself to the office.

DON'T FORGET

Ask yourself, What types of behaviors typically warrant a discipline referral in my classroom? Could (and should) I handle any of these issues myself? When I do send a student to the office, what am I hoping to accomplish? The goal, of course, should always be to help the student think about what he has done and help him to make a more mature or responsible behavior choice next time.

And remember that you are the authority figure in the classroom, the one who should handle all minor behavior problems. Only send students to the office when absolutely necessary. Be a 90 percenter!

8

A STUDENT IS DISRESPECTFUL TO YOU IN FRONT OF THE CLASS

IF THIS HAPPENS

It's an ordinary school day (if there is such a thing), and you are teaching your students. One of your students decides she doesn't like the assignment you have just given. The other students get busy, but she lets you know in no uncertain terms that she's not doing the assignment and you can't make her do it. She speaks to you in a very disrespectful tone and an elevated voice. When this happens, all of the students' eyes do not go to her. Where do they go? To *you*. Everyone is waiting to see how you will respond, including the student who just snapped at you. What will you do?

Assuming that you are a teacher who always treats your students respectfully (because if you're not, then this behavior will be quite typical in your classroom), you are taken aback. Your feelings are probably hurt, and you are also embarrassed by this student's actions. Hopefully, you are aware that you should never take a student's behavior personally. You just happened to be the nearest adult—and thus the recipient of her frustrations. Why did she do this? Maybe she's struggling with a problem outside your classroom. Maybe she's struggling with a problem inside your classroom. Maybe she's trying to show off to her friends and establish some dominance over adults. There's always a reason. But the reason does not make the behavior acceptable or permissible. What's really important at this point is not *her* behavior, but *yours*. In every classroom situation, there needs to be at least one adult—and it works best when the *teacher* is that adult.

TRY THIS

Following are tips for successful ways of dealing with a disrespectful student:

- Realize that the student is hoping to have pushed your buttons, to have engaged you in a battle of wills, and to have made you visibly upset so that everyone else can witness her power over you. Don't play her game. You'll lose every time.

- When the student displays a disrespectful behavior, resist the urge to react. Know that all eyes are on you. You have one chance to do this right.

- Speak calmly to the student. Remember—students are watching you. You're serving as a role model for handling conflict effectively. One of the best things to say is this: "I can see you're upset, so I'll wait until you calm down and speak with you afterward." (Notice that you did not ignore the behavior. Disrespect should not be ignored. Instead, you gave her time to calm down, assuring her that you will speak with her later.)

- When you do speak with her about her behavior, remain composed and professional. Avoid sounding preachy. You might say, "Wow, you seemed really upset. I know you know that your actions were disrespectful and inappropriate. What happened?" And let the student speak. Express your concern and caring. Try to identify what's bothering her.

- If there is a consequence, that's fine. Just make sure the consequence is a result of her behavior, not a result of your level of embarrassment. There's a big difference between "You acted inappropriately, so here is the logical consequence," and "You embarrassed me, so now you're going to pay for that."

- Talk with the student about how she might handle the situation differently next time. Don't assume she knows how to make a better choice in the future.

- Do not for one second let her know that she pushed your buttons or upset you personally.

- Remember that showing anger toward students is in their minds a dare to do it again. And most students will take that dare every time.

- End the conversation by smiling and saying, "Let's put this behind us and start over from here. And if you ever feel frustrated or angry about something, feel free to come to me so that we can talk about it."

DON'T FORGET

Be prepared in advance with ways you will handle disrespectful behavior. Yes, it may catch you off guard, but that's okay, because you'll know beforehand that you're going to hide your emotions and act calmly and professionally. Remember not to take a student's actions personally. If you do, you'll handle the situation ineffectively. It's not about good guy versus bad guy. It's about a student acting disrespectfully. Give the student time to cool off and then speak with her privately. If there's a consequence (as evidenced in your classroom management plan) for disrespectful behavior, then simply dole out the consequence.

Effective teachers know how to appear calm, polite, and respectful while also being firm and consistent. Students quickly learn whose buttons they *can* push and whose they *can't*. And students are much less likely to act disrespectfully toward teachers who treat them every day with respect and with dignity. This is not to suggest that disrespectful behavior never occurs in the classroom of an effective teacher. But when it does, it's treated swiftly, professionally, and effectively.

9

SOME STUDENTS ARE AFRAID TO MAKE MISTAKES

IF THIS HAPPENS

I am not discouraged, because every wrong attempt discarded is another step forward.
—THOMAS EDISON

This is an excellent quote to hang on your classroom wall, not just for your students to see, but for you, their teacher, to see. In our own teaching, we discovered, through trial and error, tons of techniques that absolutely do not work and others that absolutely do. The road to excellence is not smoothly paved! This has always been a difficult concept for many students (and many teachers) to grasp. But it's a fact of life that, if embraced, will catapult you forward, right past the pack of those who don't dare take risks because of fear of failure.

We often encounter students who are literally terrified of failure. When they do make mistakes, they don't deal with them well. Some students get angry and give up. Others simply shut down. Some refuse to even admit to making mistakes, often blaming others in their path. Have we in schools helped to nurture this fear of failure, placing far too much emphasis on getting the right answer always? And if so, what can be done to turn this around—to teach students that mistakes can contain seeds of opportunity?

TRY THIS

The following are a few ways to help students become more comfortable with taking risks and making mistakes:

- Share some of your own mistakes (along with lessons learned) with your students. Serve as a role model for making mistakes, admitting to them, and learning from them.

- Tell students about others who made mistakes and turned those mistakes into opportunity. For instance, who hasn't heard of (or used) a Post-it Note? Spencer Silver, the inventor, was attempting to develop a heavy-duty adhesive. He failed. What he got instead was a very light, easily removable adhesive that eventually led to the Post-it Note. The biologist Alexander Fleming once went on vacation, forgetting to clean plates of bacteria with which he was experimenting. He returned to discover something unusual about what was growing on the plate near the window sill. This mistake would lead to the discovery of penicillin.

- Teach students that it is *okay* to make a mistake. You can't stress this point enough. What's important is learning to recover from a mistake and using the lessons within the mistake to help you move forward.

- When a student makes a mistake, be supportive. Encourage him to find the lesson within the mistake.

- Thomas Edison also said, "I failed my way to success." Share this quote with your students and ask them what they think he meant by this. Then ask how they can apply this philosophy to their own lives.

- Create a classroom environment where it is safe for students to take risks and to make mistakes. Explain to students that it takes courage to take a risk, knowing you might make a mistake. And it takes even more courage not to allow the mistake to get the best of you, but rather to get up when you fall and try again. Remind them that no one learned to ride a bicycle on the first try! But many mistakes and a few skinned knees surely paid off in learning to ride a bicycle.

- Don't make the mistake of thinking that one lesson on making mistakes is enough. You'll have to continue to teach students how to accept and learn from their mistakes throughout the school year.

- Remember that at times it is important to reinforce the *attempt* rather than just focusing on the *result*.

DON'T FORGET

Imagine a classroom where every day teachers say, "Let's see what we can learn from our mistakes," and really mean it. An environment where successes are celebrated, but so are mistakes.

Okay, so no one celebrates making a poor grade on a test, but maybe fewer tests would result in poor grades if more teachers adopted the attitude reflected in this poem.

I MADE A MISTAKE

I tried my best and made a mistake

And my teacher thought the mistake was great

"A mistake," she said, "does not a failure make.

Do not let a problem seal your fate.

Learn from it what not to do

Then try something else and see it through."

And so I did, I continued to try.

And I made more mistakes, I can't deny

But each time I fell, I allowed the bruise

To teach me a lesson that I could use.

10

A STUDENT IS SLEEPING IN YOUR CLASS

IF THIS HAPPENS

It's an all-too familiar scene: a head falls, the eyes close, and a student enters a dream state, right in the middle of your lesson. Should you take this personally? Should you feel upset? Should you wake him or let him sleep? Should you ignore the problem? If you do, will other students follow suit and begin to use your class for nap time? If you do decide to wake him, what's the best way to do that? And once he's awake, how will you keep him awake?

Though there is no *one* technique that will solve all issues with students sleeping in class, there are several quick and easy techniques that can work remarkably well. But before you can decide which techniques to try, realize that students fall asleep in class for a variety of reasons.

Here are the most common reasons students sleep in class:

- They are bored with the content or the lesson delivery.
- They do not understand what is being taught, so they "zone out."
- They are genuinely tired due to lack of sleep, side effects of medication, or physical exhaustion from overextending themselves in after-school activities.
- They are ill.

Here are a few actions to *avoid* when a student is sleeping in class:

- Calling attention to the student in order to humiliate him.
- Acting upset about the fact that the student is sleeping.
- Startling a sleeping student.
- Punishing the student (sleeping in class is not a misbehavior, so don't treat it as one).

In considering how you will deal effectively with a student sleeping in class, you'll first have to determine the reason for the behavior. Once you've determined that, you're on your way to solving the problem.

TRY THIS

The following are some simple ways to address the issue of students sleeping in class:

- The best way to determine why a student is sleeping in class is to speak with the student privately. Express your concern and ask him about what's causing him to sleep in class and try to get to the root of the problem.
- If a student is tired due to lack of sleep, talk to him about it. Is there something within his control that he can do to assure that he begins getting more sleep? Just the fact that you express your concern about him can go a long way.
- Begin to notice patterns. Is one student sleeping, or are several students sleeping? If several students are sleeping, is it possible that this is a boring activity? If so, begin taking steps to make your activities more engaging.
- When you notice a student (or two) nodding off, provide a quick stretch break, allowing students to stand and stretch for about thirty seconds.

- If a student is tired due to the side effects of medication, you may want to speak with a parent. Sometimes a medication can be taken at a different time of day. Sometimes dosages can be adjusted. But it's important to make the parent aware that the medication is affecting his or her child's ability to stay awake in class.

- Set up *standing stations*. Why? Because it's impossible to sleep while standing. If you notice a student having trouble staying awake, allow him to do his work at the standing station—a table or platform where the student stands instead of sitting. Be careful not to treat this as a *punishment station*.

- If a student is sleeping because he is ill, send him to the office to call home.

- If you determine that a student is sleeping because he does not understand the content that you are teaching, provide remediation followed by activities tailored to his level of understanding.

- When a student nods off, stand next to him while you are teaching. You might even tap him gently and ask if he's feeling okay.

- Keep *all* of your students actively engaged and moving as much as possible.

- Remember also that prevention is always more powerful than reaction. When you see that a student is about to fall asleep, do or say something to prevent it.

DON'T FORGET

We want our students awake, because they can't learn when they are sleeping. We also want to help them if they need help—and if there is a medical issue, we want to call it to the parents' attention. If our lessons are boring, we want to spice them up. If students don't understand the way we teach, then we want to teach in a way that they understand (see Topic 41: You Teach Many Different Students at Many Different Levels). And if students aren't getting enough sleep, we want to talk to them (and maybe their parents) about possible solutions.

11

YOU LOST YOUR TEMPER WITH YOUR STUDENTS

IF THIS HAPPENS

Have you ever given in to your emotions and lost your temper with your students? Did you later find yourself regretting that loss of control, realizing it was actually counterproductive? A teacher in one of our workshops shared the following:

> I'm usually very easygoing and extremely mild-mannered. I don't ever raise my voice in anger. In fact, I've never done it until last week. The students were especially talkative, and I was, for personal reasons, especially impatient. I asked them several times to get quiet, and before I knew it, I was literally screaming at them. I have to say they were shocked. They've never seen me do this before, so my outburst definitely got their attention. I, too, was shocked. But I was already screaming, so I just kept on going. I finally ran out of steam and stopped yelling. I was embarrassed by my actions, but I didn't let them know that. For a while, I felt justified. I thought, "Hey, it worked, and they deserved it!" But in retrospect, I know that what I did was inappropriate and unprofessional. I just don't know what to do next. Should I apologize, or should I just let it go and not mention it again? Will it make me look weak if I admit that I was wrong? And will it make them feel as though they were right? Help!

This teacher might take comfort in hearing that most teachers, if they're honest, will admit to having lost their temper at one time or another with their students. Most can relate to *what* this teacher felt and *how* this teacher felt. Students can be aggravating at times. They don't always do what we want them to do. (And as we'll discuss in Topic 31: A Particular Student Is Pushing Your Buttons, they know how to get on our nerves.)

What message does it send to students when you lose your temper? It tells students that you can't control your own emotions. And if you can't control yourself, you certainly can't maintain any type of control over your students. It sends a message to students that it's okay to lose your temper when you get angry or aggravated. And that's the last message any of us wants to send to our students. It also tells students that they have power over you, because their actions caused your outburst. So is it ever appropriate to lose your temper with students? No. All situations involving students should be dealt with in a professional manner.

TRY THIS

DOWNLOAD

Here are a few tips to avoid losing your temper with your students:

- Do not allow yourself the option of losing your cool. In other words, make a commitment to yourself that no matter how irritated or aggravated you may get, you will not lose your composure.

- When you feel yourself becoming agitated with your students, recognize how you are feeling. Take a few deep breaths. If you have to walk away from the situation and pretend to busy yourself with a task, do it. Simply walk to your desk and shuffle a few papers if need be.

- Remind yourself that if you lose control of yourself, you lose control of the class.

- Fake it. This is one of the skills of great teachers. They pretend to be composed, even when they are not. They know how to speak in a calm, composed voice even when their emotions are churning and burning inside.

- Try saying to your students, "I'm upset right now and I need some time to gather my thoughts before I speak to you." It's okay to let them know you're upset with their actions. It's just not okay to lose control of yourself as a result of their actions.

Here are a few tips on what to do if you *have* lost your temper with your students:

- Regain your composure immediately. Catch yourself in the act and stop yourself.

- Wait until you are composed enough to speak calmly and rationally before addressing the fact that you lost your temper. Don't let too much time pass, however, before addressing it.

- *Always* apologize. It does not make you appear weak. On the contrary, it makes you appear strong—like someone who takes responsibility for her actions. (See Topic 4: You Embarrassed a Student in Front of His Peers for tips on how to apologize effectively.)

- Explain why you did it, but be clear that the "why" does not justify your inappropriate reaction.

- Tell what you could and should have done to handle the situation more appropriately.

DON'T FORGET

To err is human. Don't beat yourself up for past mistakes. But do realize that it's never appropriate to lose your temper with a student. Know in advance that you will sometimes be tempted to give in to your emotions. Prepare a plan for what you will do to stop yourself from giving in to those temptations. Remember: students are very forgiving, and they will accept your apology if you have lost your cool with them. But it's best to deny yourself the option of losing your cool at all.

12

YOU FEEL THAT SEVERAL OF YOUR STUDENTS ARE LAZY

IF THIS HAPPENS

The following questions were asked of both an effective and an ineffective teacher who teach the same students:

Question 1. Do you think that some students are lazy?

Ineffective Teacher: Yes. Absolutely. Many kids today expect you to do everything for them. They don't care about their schoolwork and they don't care about their grades. They sit there and do nothing. They don't do their classwork and they don't do their homework.

Effective Teacher: I don't believe there's any such thing as a lazy student. Oh, there are students who exhibit behavior that makes them appear lazy sometimes, but that's just their way of sending me a message that they're bored, they don't understand what I'm teaching, they're struggling with a problem outside of the classroom, or something else. All students want to succeed. In all of my years of teaching, I've never encountered a truly lazy student.

Question 2. What do you do if one or more students are exhibiting "lazy" behavior?

Ineffective Teacher: I tell them to get busy. If they refuse, I punish them. And if they still won't do their work, I send them to the principal. To be honest, sometimes I just ignore these students. If they don't want to learn, I can't make them. It's their choice.

Effective Teacher: The first thing I do is ask myself what I can do differently. If a student looks uninterested, I do a quick assessment to see if other students appear uninterested also. If that's the case, it usually has something to do with the current activity. If it's only one student, I talk to him or her personally to try to find out what's going on. There's always a reason, and it's my job to find out that reason so that I can start working toward a solution. Sometimes the reason stems from my teaching and other times it doesn't. But I have to figure that out first in order to know the next step to take. If the student is bored because he already knows the information I'm teaching, then I need to differentiate her instruction. If the activity is boring, I need to make it more interesting and/or engaging. If the student is struggling with personal problems, I need to lend my ear and try to help.

TRY THIS

As stated by the effective teacher, there really is no such thing as lazy students, but there are definitely students who sometimes exhibit lazy-looking behavior.

When a student exhibits "lazy" behavior, you might try the following:

- Assess the activity. Is it meaningful and engaging? And are the other students engaged? If not, change the activity.

- Consider the student's level of understanding. Is the content above her level? If so, make some adjustments by providing work for her at her current level of understanding. Is the material below her level? If the student has already mastered the content in the current activity, she may be bored. Provide her with an activity that matches her level of understanding.

- Ask the student, "Is everything okay?" Sometimes that question is enough to get the student back on track. Occasionally, a student is simply daydreaming. Other times, everything is not okay. Something is bothering the student. If this is the case, speak with the student privately and try to get to the root of the problem.

DON'T FORGET

Remind yourself that students *want* to succeed. If they appear lazy, be careful not to label them as such, even in your mind. If you think someone is lazy, you will treat her that way. This will only serve to perpetuate the behavior. When a student acts lazy, realize that the behavior is merely a symptom. Determine what's causing the symptoms so that you can treat that cause appropriately and cure the misbehavior.

13

YOU ASK A STUDENT TO STEP OUTSIDE WITH YOU AND HE REFUSES

IF THIS HAPPENS

When a student is being disruptive, it is usually best to get him away from the situation and speak with him privately. Often, it's as simple as taking the student out into the hallway for a quick one-on-one discussion. But what if you ask him to step outside with you and he refuses? A teacher shared the following with us:

> I had a student who was being disruptive in class. This particular student is often disruptive. I knew it was best to speak with him in private, so I asked him to step out into the hall with me. He responded by saying, "I'm not going anywhere!" I asked again that he step out into the hall so that I could speak with him, and again he refused. He was very disrespectful to me in front of the students. I threatened to send him to the office, and he responded that he didn't care. I then told him to go to the office, and he refused. We ended up in a screaming match, which neither of us won. I had to call for someone from the office to come and remove him from my classroom in order for me to save face.
>
> I realize I didn't handle it effectively, but I'm not sure what I should have done. I needed to speak with him privately, because I know what happens to

him when he has an audience. As it turns out, he got his audience! And I lost my temper, which was not what I had intended to do.

That scenario happens often. A student is disruptive, and a teacher tries to take the student aside in order to speak with him in private. The student refuses, and what happened in the above scenario repeats.

TRY THIS

So what can you do if you need to speak with a student privately? First, let's look at what you'll want to avoid. At all costs, avoid any type of power struggle. Both you and the student will lose, and nothing positive will be accomplished. The power struggle will cause the student to become defensive or angry, so it won't be an appropriate time to speak with him anyway. Nothing productive comes from trying to reason with a person who is too emotional to be logical. And if you are part of that power struggle, you'll be in a similar emotional state, so logic and reason won't be your strong suits either.

What can you do instead? Try this: as soon as the student begins to be disruptive, send him on an errand. Yes, an errand. Why an errand? Because students love to run errands and because running the errand will remove him from the disruptive situation. Simply send him to deliver something—anything—to the teacher right across the hall. Pretend you didn't even notice the disruptive behavior. Just calmly ask him to deliver something to the teacher across the hall. When he returns, be waiting for him at the door and speak to him calmly and rationally about the disruptive behavior. Yes, you "tricked" him, but he won't know that. You got him out into the hall, which is where you needed him to be so that you could speak with him privately. Mission accomplished. This works whether a student is in first grade or twelfth. An additional benefit is that the student's mindset is likely to be more positive than it would have been while he was in the classroom. And the minute it takes for him to deliver the note will give *you* a chance to gather your thoughts and composure.

DON'T FORGET

Here are a few points to remember when dealing with a disruptive student:

- Avoid a power struggle at all costs. No one wins.
- Once you get a chance to speak with the student privately about the disruptive behavior, remain calm, regardless of the student's reaction.
- Discuss an alternative behavior with the student—one that is more positive.
- Attack the problem, but never the person.
- Try to end the conversation on a positive note, expressing your belief in the student's ability to behave appropriately.

14

STUDENTS DON'T BRING NECESSARY SUPPLIES TO YOUR CLASS

IF THIS HAPPENS

The school year is beginning. You send the supply list home. Most students return to school with their necessary supplies. Some, however, do not. Some have their supplies the first week or two, and then they begin forgetting their supplies or leaving them in other classrooms or in the teeth of their dogs, or you name it. If we had a penny for each excuse a student has ever used for why he doesn't have his necessary supplies, we might all be wealthy! Some students always bring their supplies. Some usually do. Some never do. Some simply can't afford supplies. Others can, but still don't bring them.

A speaker was preparing to address a large audience of teachers, grades pre-K through 12. He asked all the school administrators to send a "supply list" to the teachers who would be attending the speech. The note attached to the list asked that all teachers bring to the inservice a pencil, a pen, and loose-leaf paper—three very simple supplies that all teachers have ready access to. Can you guess where this is going? About half of the 1,700 teachers in the audience arrived with all of their supplies. Half! (The rest were scrambling to "borrow" from their neighbors.) And in this case, it had nothing to do with money. They admitted that they had received the supply list. They had simply forgotten to bring what was needed. It happens.

So should you simply say, "It happens," and stop asking students to bring supplies to class? Of course not. It's perfectly acceptable to ask (and to expect) students to bring necessary supplies to class. Just try not to make a big deal out of it or get too bent out of shape when some students don't. You'll only be upsetting yourself, and you're not ever going to solve that problem completely. We do learn to pick and choose our battles, and this is a fairly insignificant battle in the grand scheme of things.

TRY THIS

The following are quotes from several teachers regarding supplies:

"I partner with a local business each year and ask for school supplies. I've found several businesses that are more than willing to keep me well stocked in basic school supplies. In return, I thank them publicly in our school newsletters and I post a sign in the room that thanks the business for its support of students. I've done this for years and have never had trouble finding a willing partner. Some of the businesses like to supply pencils advertising their business. That's fine with me! I also make a point to frequent their establishments as often as possible, encouraging students to do the same."

"I pick up supplies on the cheap at garage sales and dollar stores. I always keep a stash on hand, because I'm not going to fight that battle. Some students don't come to class prepared. They just don't. I know that in advance, so I am prepared. If a student doesn't have paper and we are doing a writing project, I still need for that student to complete his project. The alternative is to let him sit there and do nothing. That's not an option in my class."

"I have a treasure box in which I keep all kinds of fun gadgets and school supplies. Students all earn tickets in my class for a variety of reasons, and those tickets are used to buy items from the treasure chest. If a student ever comes to class without supplies, he or she is allowed to use tickets to buy supplies from the box. They don't like to waste their tickets on paper and pencils, because there are other items in the box that are much more alluring. So this helps them to remember to bring their supplies to class."

"We have a supply room for the whole school filled with common items that students (and teachers) need on a daily basis. Three local businesses provide all of the stock. Teachers are free to access the supply room at any time. We still require students to bring certain supplies on their own, but we're all realistic enough to know that some of our students won't always comply. So we have a Plan B, our supply room. It's great!"

"I simply befriended the custodian who saves all found pencils, pens, etc., for me!"

DON'T FORGET

By enlisting the support of local businesses and/or community groups, you will usually have no problem securing extra supplies for your classroom without having to spend your own money. Also, don't hesitate to send supply lists home (unless your school doesn't allow it, of course). Just realize in advance that, for a host of reasons, not all students will bring in all of their necessary supplies all of the time. You can stress out over it and get yourself tied up in knots, but that's all you'll accomplish. Have a Plan B in place and save yourself!

15

SOME STUDENTS ARE EASIER TO LIKE THAN OTHERS

IF THIS HAPPENS

Every year, you have one (or several) classes of students. And the same types of personalities seem to reemerge in each of those classes, every year. You have those who are *pleasers*. They'll do anything to please you. They work hard and do whatever is asked of them. This, of course, has nothing to do with their abilities or achievement levels. There are pleasers who make As, and there are pleasers who struggle to pass. Next, you have that middle group we'll call the *neutrals*—those students who usually behave, but not always. They're typically friendly and agreeable, but not always. They usually do their work, but not always. You have to keep your eye on them in order to ensure they are doing what is expected. Again, all ability and achievement levels are present within each group. And finally you have that group that tests your patience—the *annoyers*. They can be antagonistic, disagreeable, and downright defiant. They usually don't do what is expected of them. They're sneaky, and you're afraid to turn your back on them. From this group come strange noises, ugly gestures, inappropriate attempts at humor, and so on. Many in this group are quite intelligent and creative, and they do possess positive qualities. However, those positive qualities are often overshadowed by their annoying behaviors. A lot of them are leaders. You just hope no one is following them down their current path.

Granted, this is an oversimplified categorization of students, but any teacher can relate to the aforementioned groups. Which group is usually the most likable ? The *pleasers*, of course. Who wouldn't like someone who's nice, pleasant, polite, and agreeable? These students are easy to teach and easy to like. But do you like all pleasers the same? Of course not. Within each group, there are subgroups! But back to the three main groups. The neutrals, too, are usually fairly easy to like. You have to keep them in line from time to time, but they typically comply. And if we're honest, we can all admit that it's not always easy to like the annoyers. And yes, some of the annoyers are more annoying than other annoyers. Complicated? Not really.

Those three groups aside, let's also admit that some students, for whatever reason, are just easier to like than others. Whether it's due to their personalities or ours or a combination of both, there are a few students who are just difficult to like. No teacher likes all students the same. That's reality. But the students can never be made aware of that reality!

Great teachers pretend to like all students equally. No student in the class of a great teacher feels slighted, because every student is treated as if he or she is the teacher's favorite. Therein is the secret. All students in the class of a great teacher believe that the teacher genuinely likes them, respects them, and cares about them. That is why the *annoyers* are much less annoying in the classrooms of great teachers. In fact, it's sometimes difficult to distinguish in the classroom of a great teacher which students would fall into which category. The lines become blurred, and that is a very good thing.

TRY THIS

First, be honest with yourself. Aren't there some students you like a little more than others? That's okay, because you're human. But again, students can't ever be made aware that you like some more than others. If an annoyer ever figures out that you like others more than you like him, he will very likely become more annoying. And the more annoyed you act with him, the more annoying he becomes. It's a vicious cycle.

Can you simply ignore annoying behaviors? Though many behaviors can be ignored, others cannot. You know the difference. If a student exhibits a behavior that cannot be ignored, deal with it. But do so in a way that says, "I like you, but your behavior is unacceptable. There is a consequence to your actions." Deal with him calmly and professionally, and let it go. Do *not* take the behavior personally. Teachers run into problems when they wear their emotions on their sleeves, effectively announcing that the students are controlling their teachers' emotions.

What many fail to realize is that there are subtle, clever ways of defusing an annoyer, such as the following:

- Try to find out why the student is behaving inappropriately by speaking with her privately. Express your concern and your willingness to help. Approach her with a calm demeanor.

- Act as though you know the student does not want to act this way, especially in front of her peers. Let her know you are willing to help her learn to behave differently.

- Tell her that you like her—you like her a lot. And because you like her, you want to help her behave more responsibly and appropriately.

- Find genuine ways to praise the student when she is behaving well. This in itself can work wonders to deter inappropriate behavior.

- Be patient, and remind yourself, as soon as the annoyer displays an annoying behavior, not to act out of frustration or aggravation.

- Make a special effort every day to treat all students as if they are your favorites. This sounds easy, but it's not. It is, however, necessary.

DON'T FORGET

- Identify in your mind the students you like least in each class you teach.

- Begin today to find ways to praise them, to give them small jobs to do for you, and to win them over with your kindness and caring.

- If a behavior can be ignored, ignore it. If it cannot be ignored, approach it professionally and calmly.

- Always leave the student with the message that you care about her as opposed to being outdone by her.

- Make every effort to convince each student that she is your favorite. It's not difficult to do. If you make an effort to show interest in a student and you treat her fairly and kindly, she will think she's your favorite.

16

A STUDENT IS PRONE TO ANGRY OUTBURSTS

IF THIS HAPPENS

Some children learn that when they throw a tantrum, they eventually get what they want. (Remember: no one repeats a behavior without a reward.) We've all witnessed this in the supermarket, haven't we? And these children eventually become students in our classrooms.

Basically, angry outbursts can come from two types of students: (1) students who are emotionally and/or behaviorally challenged and (2) students who sometimes struggle to express their emotions appropriately.

With the first type of student—a student who has already been diagnosed with a behavior exceptionality—there should already be a behavior plan in place. In this section, we'll be addressing the second type of student: the student who simply struggles to express his emotions appropriately.

The following are behaviors you might witness from students who are prone to angry outbursts:

- A reaction from a student that is disproportionate to the event that caused the outburst
- A temper tantrum that may involve crying or screaming
- Lashing out at others, including classmates or teachers
- Using verbally abusive language

- Throwing objects
- Slamming fists on desk
- Threatening to hurt others
- Destroying his own property or the property of others
- Angrily refusing to do work in class

At one time or another, all teachers encounter such outbursts from students. And all teachers want to do what's best—for the student and for the rest of the class.

TRY THIS

The following are actions you will want to *avoid* when a student displays an angry outburst:

- Avoid losing your temper with the student. This will serve to escalate an already volatile situation. Arguing with a student is like mud wrestling with a pig. You both get dirty, but only the pig enjoys it!
- Avoid trying to reason with an angry student. It won't work, ever. Give him time and space to regain his composure.
- Avoid the temptation to enforce an immediate consequence. Again, allow the student time to calm down.
- Do not argue with an angry student, even in a controlled voice.
- Do not touch an angry student.

The following are quick steps to help defuse an angry student:

- Display a calm demeanor, regardless of how you feel on the inside. This will help defuse an angry student.
- Look for early warning signs and try to nip the problem in the bud before it escalates.

- Try speaking soothing words to the student. For instance, you might say, "I know you're upset, so take a deep breath and we'll talk about it after you calm down."

- Sometimes it is best to avoid any type of immediate response. If you see that the student is running out of steam, let him. You can deal with him more effectively after he has lost his momentum.

Note: If the student is endangering other students, it is your first priority to keep those students safe. Call for assistance if you cannot handle the situation on your own.

After the student has calmed down, try the following:

- Speak with the student about what happened. Try to determine the cause. If at all possible, deal with the situation on your own. If a pattern develops, however, you may want to meet with your administrator to discuss enlisting the support of parents, school counselors, or others.

- Discuss with the student how he could have acted more appropriately. Provide several options for him if he cannot come up with ideas on his own.

- It is okay to attach a consequence to an angry outburst. If you do decide to give the student a consequence, do so in a calm manner.

- Let the student know in advance of the consequence he can expect to face if the behavior is repeated. Explain again appropriate ways to deal with feelings of anger.

- After a few days, you may want to meet with the student again to ask how things are going and to remind him again of appropriate ways to deal with feelings of anger. Role play works well in such situations. Give the student a few scenarios and discuss both appropriate and inappropriate ways to deal with each scenario.

DON'T FORGET

Any time a student has an angry outburst, your initial response will play a vital role in either escalating or de-escalating the situation. Remember to appear calm and to allow the student to calm down before you address the situation. If others are at risk of being harmed, your response to the situation will, of course, have to be immediate.

There is always an underlying cause for angry outbursts, but regardless of that cause, the behavior is unacceptable. Make sure that the student knows that the behavior is unacceptable and why it is unacceptable. Don't assume that he already knows this.

If the problem becomes chronic with a particular student, enlist the support of both parents and school support personnel—an administrator, a social worker, a psychologist, or a counselor. Develop a plan for what to do if the behavior is repeated in the future. If the student has a tendency to become violent, have a plan in place for removing him from the environment quickly and efficiently. This has to be planned beforehand. Most situations, however, can be dealt with quickly and effectively by the teacher in the classroom.

> I've come to a frightening conclusion that I am the decisive element in the classroom. It's my personal approach that creates the climate. It's my daily mood that makes the weather. As a teacher, I possess a tremendous power to make a child's life miserable or joyous. I can be a tool of torture or an instrument of inspiration. I can humiliate or heal. In all situations, it is my response that decides whether a crisis will be escalated or de-escalated and a child humanized or dehumanized.
>
> —HAIM G. GINOTT

17

IT'S DIFFICULT TO STAY MOTIVATED WHEN THE STUDENTS AREN'T MOTIVATED

IF THIS HAPPENS

How motivated were you during your first year of teaching? How motivated are you now? Have you become more or less enthusiastic about teaching over the course of your career? J. B., a high school teacher, shared the following:

I had really sunken to an all-time low in my teaching. I had adopted the "lazy-kid" rhetoric and practically given up. Oh, I was still doing my job, technically, but I had begun putting about as much effort into my teaching as my students seemed to be putting into their learning. This had all happened, of course, over a period of time. So I honestly didn't even realize how negative I had become until it was almost too late. A chance encounter with a former student would bring the old Mr. B, the enthusiastic, fun-loving, effective teacher, back to life. I was in the hardware store when I heard, "Mr. B, is that you?" It was Monica, a student I had taught many years ago. She said, "You were my favorite teacher. I still remember when you used to . . ." And she went on to name specific activities from my class, off-the-wall things I had done, old corny jokes I used to tell, etc. She said, "You were the nicest, funniest teacher I ever knew. You made learning so much fun. Everybody wanted to be in your class!" Needless to say, I couldn't sleep that night. Her words had humbled and haunted me. She had described an actual person—the person I used to be. Where had that person gone? I knew, beyond doubt, that none of my students today would think I was fun or positive or even nice. I knew it was no longer true that everyone wanted to be in my class. In fact, I was fairly certain most of my students dreaded my class these days.

Instead of beating myself up, I did what I was taught to do early on in my teaching—and what I used to teach my students to do—learn from your mistakes, let them go, and move on! I was determined to recapture that unbridled enthusiasm for teaching and learning that used to be mine. I resolved to be a new person—the old person—the next day. I went to school and smiled at everyone I met. My students, I have to admit, appeared shocked. But I can guarantee that everyone noticed! I pretended to be the happiest man in the world, and I acted as though everything I taught was the most exciting thing my students would ever learn. I did this for a day, then for a week, and then for the rest of the year. I've continued to do it ever since. And guess what! I no longer complain about my students' lack of motivation, because I work really hard to ensure that I keep them motivated. Even on days when my mood isn't the greatest, I just pretend that it is. To make a long story short, I'm the favorite teacher in the school again—just the way I used to be! Students can't wait to come to my class each day, and I make sure I don't let them down. Student attitudes are so much better when the teacher has a great attitude. I'm living proof of that!

TRY THIS

Does this sound familiar? Have you ever found yourself feeling like you've lost your own enthusiasm for teaching and for motivating yourself and your students? What J. B. realized, thanks to his encounter with a former student, was that he was the one who had lost his enthusiasm and fire. You see, if your own fire isn't burning, the students' fires surely won't be. You have to be motivated *first*, or at least you have to *act* motivated first. As the old saying goes, "Many people who say they are burned out were never on fire to begin with!"

But how do you ignite that fire? How do your reclaim your passion for teaching?

- First, you'll have to recognize your lack of enthusiasm and then be resigned to overcome it. Don't fall into the role of victim. Remember: we all signed up for this profession. No one made us do it. We chose teaching to make a difference. Motivating an unmotivated student makes a *huge* difference!

- Do what J. B. did. *Decide* to act in a more positive, enthusiastic manner with your students. Fake it 'til you make it. Pretend that everything you teach is your favorite thing to teach.

- Surround yourself with positive coworkers. We can all benefit from a dose of someone else's enthusiasm every day. It's contagious!

- Avoid negative coworkers who try to bring others down with them.

- Connect with other positive educators using social media.

- Keep a file of thoughts or inspirational quotes that inspire you and read them when you most need them.

- Change some of the scenery in your room. Brighten things up.

- Find out specifically from your students what motivates them and how they enjoy learning best. Then incorporate some of what you have learned into your teaching. The very fact that you asked for their input will help them to see that you care and are making an attempt to make learning more enjoyable and meaningful for them.

- Ensure that your students know you value them as people, and make an effort to find out what they value in life. Students who feel valued by their teachers display more motivation than those who do not.

- Set high, yet reasonable, expectations for your students and then assist them in meeting those expectations. Success is one of the *best* motivators of all. Unsuccessful students are not likely to be motivated by their failures. If a task is not "doable," then where's the motivation to actually do it?

- Introduce a little friendly competition into some of your activities. Again, make the task challenging yet doable.

- Plan activities that are fun, meaningful, and engaging.

- Allow students to work with partners or in groups.

- Become your students' biggest cheerleader.

DON'T FORGET

Begin to notice that once your enthusiasm spills over onto your students, theirs will in turn spill onto you. It's a wonderful cycle. The reverse—lack of motivation—can be a vicious cycle. Break it.

Once students feel successful, they will be more motivated. Knowing that you helped to motivate them will help *you* to be more motivated. But you're going to have to get that ball rolling, and you're going to have to keep it rolling with your ongoing support, enthusiasm, belief in your students, and passion for making a difference.

PART TWO

Challenges with Adults

18

SOME OF YOUR COWORKERS ARE NEGATIVE

IF THIS HAPPENS

They're in every school—the "human vacuums" that can suck the life out of you with their ever-looming negativity. They are victims, in their minds, of parents, students, administrators, education policies, and life. You already know before you encounter them today that their body language will be negative and their words even more so. You dread any such encounter, but crossing their path is inevitable. When you do meet up with them in the hallway, in a meeting, or in the lounge, they're practically in your face, anxious to bend your ear with the latest gossip or the newest complaint. You have found yourself taking a longer route to your classroom or to the office or to the lunchroom, in a desperate attempt to circumvent such an encounter. When committees are selected, you utter silent prayers that they will not be on yours. You've actually hidden in your own classroom to avoid these people. But they always find you, don't they? And when they do find you, you don't quite know what to say or how to handle them. You walk away feeling exhausted. They *can* have a negative effect on you.

You don't want to be negative and you don't want to be in the company of people who drain you emotionally. You're a positive, dedicated teacher. But it's easy and sometimes even tempting to get sucked in with the naysayers. Don't do it. There's nothing good—nothing—that can possibly come of adding any negativity to any school setting. The students deserve to be in the company of positive professionals each and every day. You know this, and you're determined to maintain your positive outlook. But how do you do so?

TRY THIS

Here are a few simple ways to deal with negative coworkers effectively:

- When a negative coworker approaches you, try smiling before they even begin speaking. Be very careful not to mirror their negative body language or tone. The last thing a negative person wants is to remain in the company of an upbeat, positive person.

- Approach the negative coworker with compassion and concern. When he or she complains about something, say things like, "I'm so sorry that happened. Is there anything I can do to help?" You're not agreeing. You're simply being compassionate. This will often defuse a negative person.

- Remember not to take the actions of negative coworkers personally. They're not only being negative with you or about you. They're doing this with everyone.

- Don't participate. Then you become an enabler. These people are like fires that need fuel in order to continue to burn. Take away the fuel, and the fire dies. These negative people are fueling their own flames with the help of others. Don't be one of those "others."

- When you find yourself in conversation with a negative coworker, try to keep the conversation light. If you work with this person, you probably already know some of his or her hot-button topics. Steer clear of any of those.

- If a negative coworker is sharing a problem and you feel you have a possible solution, ask, "Do you mind if I offer a possible solution?"

- Change the subject completely.

- Avoid being around these people whenever possible. You may not have control over where you sit at a math department meeting, but you do have control over whom you sit with to eat lunch.

- Be sure to speak well of students, parents, and the school when you are in the company of negative coworkers.

- Praise negative coworkers. Say something like, "That's a great color on you," or "I'm glad you're on the committee, because I'll be depending on you to help me come up with some positive solutions to our challenges."

- Enlist the support of other positive coworkers and agree that you will all be nothing but positive in the company of these negative people. It's actually quite fun to watch what happens when you do this. You literally stun them!

DON'T FORGET

Regardless of your mood, even when you are not feeling particularly upbeat, remember to be overly kind and positive when you are in the company of negative coworkers. This makes them very uncomfortable, because misery does love company. They'll soon see you as a dead end and will seek comfort elsewhere. Negative people can be poisonous to the work environment when they are allowed to do nothing but gripe and complain. The aforementioned simple techniques can be a perfect antidote for counteracting negativism. And remember that there's power in numbers. Hang out with the positive crowd and use your positive attitudes to derail your negative coworkers.

19

YOU EXPERIENCE A LACK OF PARENTAL INTEREST

IF THIS HAPPENS

We hear it (and maybe even say it) often: some parents don't seem to care. They don't participate in their children's education, they don't volunteer to help at school, they don't return letters that require their signatures, and they won't even answer phone calls.

Have you found yourself wishing that the parents of your students would participate more actively in the education of their children? And if so, is there anything you can do?

Though it is true that some parents don't participate as actively as we'd like them to, it is unfair to say that parents don't care. Most of them genuinely do. They want the best for their children. So why do so many of them avoid any contact with the school that their children attend?

Some parents are intimidated by teachers and administrators. For years, they have only received negative messages about their children. So they begin avoiding all contact with the school. They look the other way and hope the problems will go away. Other parents avoid contact with the school due to their own unpleasant memories of school. Understanding this is the first step to establishing a more positive relationship with the parents of the students we teach.

TRY THIS

DOWNLOAD

Some teachers have tremendous success in communicating with parents. Here are a few of their secrets:

- At the beginning of the school year, send a letter or e-mail of welcome to parents telling them a little about yourself and the subject(s) you will be teaching. Thank them for the privilege of teaching their children.

- Every day send at least one quick note (two sentences maximum) telling a parent about something good his or her child has done today. Make sure every student's parents receive this type of note every few weeks. It takes about a minute of your time each day, and it's time well spent. If parents become accustomed to receiving positive messages about their children, they will be much more likely to work with you when their child is having a problem at school.

- Send an occasional class letter or group e-mail to parents, telling them about exciting things that are happening in your classroom.

- Make occasional positive phone calls to parents about their children. If they don't answer, simply leave a message saying, "I'm proud of Trish because she did really well on her science project, and I just wanted to share that good news with you."

- Have students write a quick note to their parents. For instance, you may have Craig write a note telling his parents that he has been doing much better working independently at his computer station. He writes the note, and then you simply sign it at the bottom. These notes almost always find their way home.

- Set up a class website or social media account that parents can access (many schools do this). On this site, post updates of positive happenings in your classroom. You can also post homework assignments, due dates for projects, photos of students working, and so forth.

- When you have to confer with a parent regarding a problem with his child, be sure to begin and end on a positive note. Tell the parents about the positive attributes you recognize and appreciate in his child. Compliment the parent on his willingness to attend the meeting. If a parent is angry or defensive, never respond in kind. Remain calm and professional and tell the parent you want to work cooperatively with him to do what's best for the child.

DON'T FORGET

When parents don't participate in the education of their children, there's always a reason. Believe it or not, some parents have never received anything but negative communication from their child's school. Reach out first with positive communication to the parents of your students. That alone will increase the likelihood of their cooperation and assistance if problems arise with their children. We want to *build* a relationship before we *need* a relationship.

Will the aforementioned suggestions get all parents to participate? No. But you should see some immediate results from many parents you may have written off as uncaring or unwilling.

A ninth-grade English teacher shared the following:

I make it a point to establish positive communication with my students' parents every year. I figured out many years ago that if you can convince a parent that you're a partner and not a threat, and that you care about his child, he will do almost anything to help you. Fellow teachers complain about the very same parents, saying the parents won't communicate with them. But that's because they only attempt to make contact when the student is in trouble. I deal with the same parents, and I have nothing but cooperation from them. The secret is in how you approach them!

20

YOU DISAGREE WITH YOUR ADMINISTRATOR

IF THIS HAPPENS

Jeni was an excellent teacher. Her friend Russ was not quite as excellent. His actions at times bordered on unprofessional. If he thought something, it came out of his mouth, and not always in the most tactful of ways. They taught across the hall from one another. Together, they came up with an idea. As a way to increase student motivation, they devised an incentive program. They wanted to host a party at the end of each grading period for any student who showed improvement in effort and grades. The idea was that if a student put forth more effort (as evidenced by the guidelines they had set) and improved at least one letter grade from his or her previous report card in at least one subject, he or she would be invited to the party. For students who already had high grade point averages, the idea was that they had to maintain the average and show improved effort and participation in class.

Jeni and Russ approached the principal with their idea. The principal immediately said he would not allow them to do this. He felt there was already enough "play time, reward time, and partying" in the school. He wanted to see less of that, not more. Upon hearing the principal's decision, Russ became angry. He lashed out at the principal, basically saying the principal was wrong, he didn't want to allow his teachers to try anything new, and he obviously didn't care about the students. He stormed out of the principal's office with righteous indignation. Jeni, always the professional, was left feeling embarrassed by Russ's actions. She said, "I'm so sorry that happened. But do you mind if I share my rationale behind this new idea?" The principal had always respected Jeni, and he was more than happy to continue to speak with her after Russ had left. Jeni explained that she simply wanted to try this as an experiment to see if the idea had any merit. She explained that she had devised the plan with a goal that she felt was attainable for all students. The party, she explained, would last only an hour. But if students worked harder the entire grading period for a simple one-hour reward, she felt it would be an hour well spent. "Could we try it just for one grading period? If less than half of the students don't meet the requirements to attend the party, I'll agree that that will be the end of it. We won't do it again for the next grading period."

Long story short, the principal agreed to allow the incentive program for one grading period. If it worked, they could continue with it. If not, they would abandon it. The incentive program worked—more than two-thirds of Jeni's class attended the party. The principal was thrilled with the results. The incentive program has continued to this day. The whole school now participates.

It's important to note that both Jeni and Russ wanted the same thing. Upon first hearing the idea, the principal was reluctant to allow it. He gave his reasons, and Russ reacted unprofessionally. Jeni, on the other hand, asked to explain her rationale. When the principal learned more about it and understood it better, he was willing to allow Jeni to experiment. But even if he had not allowed either teacher to implement the idea, Russ would have still been wrong in his actions. Even in times of disagreement, it's not okay to act unprofessionally.

TRY THIS

If you find yourself in disagreement with your administrator, try the following:

- Think about why you disagree. Sometimes you'll realize that your administrator is right. If this happens, tell the administrator that you realize he was right. That's what a professional does.

- If you believe that your administrator is wrong about something, take some time to meet with the administrator and state your case professionally, not argumentatively. Even if the administrator doesn't see things your way, you have still done the right thing by acting professionally. You won't always agree. That's just a fact of life.

- Never bad-mouth your administrator to other coworkers. This kind of talk will usually get back to the administrator. But even if it doesn't, it will only serve to make you appear bitter and unprofessional.

- Don't just come to your administrator with arguments as to why you disagree with him. Instead, state your case with reasons, with data, and with solutions to a particular problem.

- If after speaking with your administrator you still disagree, then just agree to disagree and let it go. It doesn't necessarily mean that someone is right and someone is wrong. Sometimes it simply means that you disagree with one another.

- Don't hold a grudge against your administrator. Holding a grudge is a sure way to poison any relationship, professional or personal.

DON'T FORGET

It's okay to disagree with your administrator. Professional people do this all the time. No teacher always agrees with his administrator on all decisions. But true professionals always act professionally, even in times of disagreement. When you find yourself disagreeing with your administrator, don't tell everyone else about it. Instead, go to the source and hold a calm, professional conversation. You may not always get the results you want, but you'll be able to respect yourself for handling the situation maturely, honestly, and responsibly. Sometimes you'll get the results you wanted. Other times you'll just have to agree to disagree.

21

YOU WANT TO FIT IN WITH THE FACULTY

IF THIS HAPPENS

Kendra was a new teacher. She was really excited about her new job and was anxious to get to know her new coworkers. She considered herself to be very easy to get along with, and she thought she would have no problem fitting in. Soon these people would be her new family—her work family.

Before the end of her first week, Kendra had met and visited with everyone on the faculty. Some, she sought out; others sought her first. But something was quite obvious to Kendra. Not everyone on the faculty got along with everyone else on the faculty. There were actually three groups. There was one group that was positive, upbeat, and enthusiastic. They warmly welcomed her to the school and offered any help they could provide. They also said they were eager to get to know her and learn from her. Teachers who fell into the second group were not too negative and not too positive. They did not appear to be very enthusiastic about anything involving their jobs. They seemed nice enough, just uninterested or disconnected in some way. And the third group was *very* interested in winning Kendra over, warning her of all that was wrong with the students, the parents, the administration, and teaching in general. They were very vocal in warning her of which teachers, administrators, students, and parents she should avoid. They seemed overly eager to take her under their protective wings.

Sadly, Kendra's story is far too recognizable. And oftentimes new teachers accidentally "fall in" with the wrong teachers in their zeal to "fit in." On an added note, this dilemma is not reserved only for new teachers.

TRY THIS

Whether you're a new or "old" teacher, these tips apply to anyone wanting to fit in while being careful not to fall in:

- Be a walking billboard for true professionalism.

- Be nice to everyone, but don't engage in idle gossip or participate in any negative chatter.

- Associate with positive, professional teachers. Though it will be tempting at times to "get a little sympathy" or possibly "share a little misery" (as we discussed in Topic 18: Some of Your Coworkers Are Negative), don't allow yourself to do it.

- Do a lot of listening. Others like to be heard. Good listening skills will get you far in life. And remember that "listening" and "agreeing" don't always go hand in hand.

- Participate in faculty gatherings whenever possible. This helps to cement your place in the "family."

- Do your part. When appropriate, offer your assistance. Let others see that you are a committed, dedicated, hard-working, caring individual.

- Be very clear about which group you most want to fit in with.

- Don't obsess over who on the faculty likes you. Though it is important to be a team player, being popular among the faculty is not why you chose teaching. Always keep the students as your main priority.

DON'T FORGET

You won't fit in with everyone unless everyone is on the same page—and they won't be. So pick the ones you want to be most like—the positive, professional teachers, right? Those are the ones whose respect you'll want to earn. And you will earn it, by being positive and professional. The middle group will accept you too, though they may not buy into all of your energy and enthusiasm. The other group will be intimidated by you, as they're intimidated by all their other positive coworkers. Kill 'em with kindness, but don't join in any reindeer games with them.

22

A COWORKER SAYS SOMETHING NEGATIVE ABOUT YOU

IF THIS HAPPENS

Two teachers, Barbara and Melinda, are chatting during the lunch break. Mrs. Warn-the-Others happens upon their conversation, eager to share her latest news. "I figured you'd want to know that Mrs. Groucher is saying unkind things about you both. She's saying you're the principal's two pets and that you stoop to very low levels to get whatever you want from him. She also says you two get to hand-pick your students, and that's why you don't have to send students to the office for discipline problems." As she's about to share even more negative chatter, the bell rings. All three go off to their respective classrooms.

Barbara thinks to herself, "I guess poor Mrs. Groucher needs to speak ill of someone, and today it was my turn. What she said is not true, of course, but I certainly am not going to defend myself when I've got nothing to defend. I'm glad she has at least noticed that I handle my own discipline problems. Maybe she's a little intimidated by that fact. I'll be overly kind the next time I see her."

Melinda thinks to herself, "How dare she! I do *not* stoop to any level to obtain favors. And I am not the principal's pet. I can't help it if he likes me. I'm a good teacher, so why wouldn't he like me? And no, I don't send students to the office, but it's not because I hand-pick my students. I've never hand-picked even one student! Why would she say that? I'm sorry, but I'm not letting her get away with this." At the end of the day, Melinda confronts Mrs. Groucher. Mrs. Groucher, of course, denies saying anything negative. Nonetheless, harsh words are spoken, professionalism is compromised, feelings are hurt, and both walk away angry. Melinda feels even worse now, because she knows Mrs. Groucher is lying to her. She'll find a way to prove it! She goes home and calls Barbara. Barbara tells her not to lose any sleep over it. Mrs. Groucher is negative, and everyone knows it. No one listens to her anyway. Melinda cannot believe that Barbara is not as outraged as she is. Oh well, she's going to have to go it alone. But she has to protect her reputation, and she is simply not going to let Mrs. Groucher off the hook. She now faces a long, sleepless night as she contemplates how to win a losing battle.

TRY THIS

First, realize that you work in a place with lots of other people. And sometimes even adults can act inappropriately and say hurtful things about each other. But when someone says something negative about you, remember that you have a choice in how you react. You can't control what they say about you, but you can certainly control your actions thereafter. Barbara realized this. Melinda did not.

Barbara considered the source and decided that this was nothing to lose sleep over. She thought about the fact that Mrs. Groucher is negative, and she actually felt a little pity for poor Mrs. Groucher. She quickly decided that her best course of action was no action at all, aside from being extra kind to Mrs. Groucher when she next saw her.

Melinda took Mrs. Groucher's words to heart and allowed those empty words to fill her with anxiety and indignation. She did what Mrs. Groucher wanted her to do—she took the bait. As a result, she lost her cool, compromised her professionalism, and entered into a futile power struggle. Who knows how long this battle will last. One thing, however, is certain—Melinda has already lost.

DON'T FORGET

No one's words or actions should ever make you compromise your professionalism. When someone says something negative about you, it's usually best not to fuel the flame. Consider the source, and notice that negative people tend to speak negatively about anyone and everyone. Others know this, and they rarely listen to these people. Well, the other negative people listen attentively, but again, consider the source. It is usually best to leave it alone and ignore the negative chatter, even if it's about you. However, if you feel strongly that you must address the issue, think about what you will say and how you will say it in advance. Then approach that person in a calm manner. Do this, of course, in private. And maintain your professionalism no matter what. A good rule is to treat everyone with such respect and dignity that if others say something negative about you, no one will believe them.

You can't control what others do. You can only be in control of you!

23

YOUR PRINCIPAL GIVES YOU A NEGATIVE EVALUATION

IF THIS HAPPENS

It happens to many, and for a variety of reasons: a teacher receives an unfavorable evaluation from the principal based on an observation. No teacher wants to receive negative results. We all want to do well, both on days when we are being observed and on days when we are not. But we all need and deserve honest feedback on our current performance in the classroom.

Yes, the truth can sometimes hurt. Sometimes, a negative evaluation is warranted. Other times it is not. Both will be addressed here, as we take a look at (1) what you can do if you receive a negative evaluation that was accurate and (2) what you can do if you receive such an evaluation that you feel is not accurate.

Upon receiving an unfavorable evaluation, the first thing you should do, of course, is to take a deep breath and view your evaluation results as objectively as possible. Go through the results point by point. For instance, if you scored poorly on an item stating that your objective was not written in clear, measureable terms and you realize that in fact it was *not* written in clear, measureable terms (as evidenced by your lesson plan), then the principal was correct on that point. There's no logical argument there. If, however, your objective was, in your opinion, written in clear, measureable terms, you will want to address this with your principal.

TRY THIS

What you might consider doing if you receive a negative evaluation that was accurate:

- Understand that no one wants to receive negative evaluation results, so it is normal to feel upset.

- If the evaluation results are accurate, and you can agree that your lesson did not go well, you may want to give yourself some time to study the results and plan how you will address these results with your principal.

- Give yourself some time to calm down and compose your thoughts. Go through the evaluation point by point. If you know how you can improve on each point, write a plan for improvement. If you don't know how you can improve on one or more points, ask your principal for help in doing so.

- Schedule a meeting with your principal to discuss your thoughts about the evaluation. Bring your plan for improvement, your questions, and any other thoughts or ideas you would like to discuss. A principal will respond much more favorably to a teacher who recognizes her own shortcomings and devises a plan for improvement than he will to a teacher who defends her actions and appears bitter and victimized. If he has valid points regarding things you did that were not effective, admit it and agree with him.

- State your case professionally. Maybe you had a legitimate reason for scoring poorly in a particular area like classroom management. Maybe you had asked the principal weeks ago for help with classroom management. The principal had promised to bring a master teacher in to help you and had forgotten to do so. Your argument here would be valid. In this case, maybe the principal will agree to provide you with some help and then reevaluate your classroom management after you have received that help.

- Make it clear to your principal that you want to improve and will work diligently to do so.

- Remain professional throughout the meeting. Ask questions and feel free to take notes. Ask for suggestions on how your principal feels you could improve in any areas of weakness.

- It's okay to discuss your strengths with your principal. Point out what you feel you did well. If he did not point out any of your strengths in the evaluation, ask him what strengths he noticed and ask him to add notes on those strengths to the evaluation.

- Following the meeting, you may want to document your improvement efforts and share that documentation with your principal so that he sees you are working at improving. Invite your principal to return to your classroom to witness that improvement.

- Don't be too hard on yourself. No teacher is perfect. Instead, commit to improving and celebrate your accomplishments. You may want to enlist the support of a trusted coworker, a mentor teacher, or anyone else who can help you to improve in your areas of weakness.

Following are things you might consider doing if you receive a negative evaluation that you feel was inaccurate:

- Wait until you are calm enough and composed enough to speak to your principal rationally.

- Go through every item on the evaluation that you disagree with, point by point.

- Ask your principal to explain why he thought you were ineffective in each area. Also ask what he thought you could or should have done differently. Then state your case and say why you disagree.

- Take notes about what is discussed during this meeting, because documentation is important, especially if you may be contesting these evaluation results.

- Keep your emotions out of any notes or letters you may send to someone else in the chain of command. You don't want to appear anything other than professional.

- It is possible that after you state your case the principal may revise the evaluation results. For instance, maybe you were able to clarify something he did not understand during the lesson. If, however, the principal still feels that his evaluation is accurate, let him know that you respectfully disagree.

- If, after you meet with your principal, you are still unsatisfied with the evaluation results, the next step is to take your concerns to the next person in the chain of command.

DON'T FORGET

Whether you agree or disagree with your unfavorable evaluation results, remain composed, professional, and as objective as possible. Speak to your principal about your results and determine where the two of you agree and disagree. If you can agree that you need improvement in certain areas, devise a plan to address each point of weakness and let your principal know you are committed to improving. If you do not agree with areas of weakness that the principal noted on the evaluation, ask questions and state reasons why you feel his evaluation was inaccurate. If you're still not satisfied, take your concerns to the next person in the chain of command.

A final word of caution: don't discuss your grievance with other teachers. They can't do anything about it other than to share what you told them with others. Soon the word is out to everyone. In this case, whether you're right or wrong, you will appear unprofessional.

24

A PARENT WILL NOT RETURN YOUR CALL

IF THIS HAPPENS

A particular student has become out of control. His behavior has gone from bad to worse, his grades are poor, and you recognize that he is in a downward spiral. You want to inform his mother of what's happening, hopefully enlisting her support. You feel as though you've done all you can at school, and you're just not getting results. So you decide to call her. You get her voicemail, and you leave a message asking her to return your call. Two days go by, and no return phone call. You call a second time, and later a third. No response. It's obvious that she is avoiding speaking with you.

So what can you do? Hopefully, this is not the first time you attempt to contact this parent. Remember that in Topic 19 (You Experience a Lack of Parental Interest) we discussed the importance of maintaining ongoing, positive communication with parents and provided tips to help you accomplish that.

Regardless, things are what they are at this point. So don't bemoan what you have or have not yet done. Just take an honest assessment of your previous communication with this parent and use that knowledge to help you move forward from here.

TRY THIS

Here are a few things to consider when attempting to contact a parent regarding a problem with his or her child:

- Before you attempt to contact the parent, be clear on what the problem is, what you have done thus far to deal with it, and what you are hoping the parent can do to aid in finding a solution.

- Look at the contact information you have for each parent. Sometimes there are multiple contact numbers—and often more than one caregiver living in separate households. If you cannot contact person A, try person B.

- Be careful about what you say (and how you say it) in your voicemail, e-mail, or handwritten communication with parents. You want to appear concerned rather than intimidating.

- Ask other teachers who also teach the student if they have had success in contacting this parent. Sometimes others, even the secretary or school receptionist, can help shed light on such a situation.

- When a parent neglects to return you phone calls, don't take it personally. At all costs, leave your personal emotions out of this. Your goal is to help the student, period.

- Talk to the student. Let him know you are trying to help him and that you are trying to contact his parent. Don't use this as a threat, as in, "If you don't shape up, I'm calling your mother." In that case, he'll do everything in his power to stop his mother from connecting with you.

- If you make several attempts to reach a parent by phone to no avail, you may want to send a carefully worded e-mail. Some parents are more likely to respond to an e-mail message than they are to a phone call. Though it's not ideal, and though a face-to-face meeting might be best, you may have to settle for electronic communication.

- Realize that you may never hear from the parent, despite your best efforts. In that case you'll have to deal with the issue at school, without the support of the parent.

- If necessary, take the problem to your administrator and ask for guidance and/or assistance. If the problem is serious enough, your administrator may choose to make a home visit.

- Document all of your attempts to contact this parent.

DON'T FORGET

Realize that once you have exhausted all of your resources, the parent's response (or lack of response) is out of your control. But the student is yours to teach and to reach every day. Be careful not to fall into the trap of "Well, his parents won't help, so my hands are tied." In fact, step up your efforts to let him know you care, you are concerned, you are willing to help, and you will not give up on him.

25

YOU'RE AFRAID TO SPEAK YOUR MIND IN A FACULTY MEETING

IF THIS HAPPENS

So you go to the weekly faculty meetings and you just sort of observe. There are always discussions relevant to students, parents, the curriculum, current programs, and the everyday business of teaching. During these discussions you are often tempted to share your ideas, feelings, and opinions. Yet you're afraid to speak up. You rationalize your silence by telling yourself that no one really listens anyway, that it's always the same people who take over the discussions (the negative people), that you don't have enough years on the faculty to be respected by everyone, and so forth. You can rationalize away, but if you dig deep enough, you'll soon realize that those reasons don't justify your silence—especially if what you have to say could benefit students.

TRY THIS

If you find yourself reluctant to speak your mind in a faculty meeting, ask yourself the following questions:

- What is it that is keeping me from sharing my ideas or opinions in a meeting?

- Am I afraid to be unpopular with the people who may disagree with me?

- Do I feel that what I have to say is valid, or do I lack faith in my own opinions?

- What do I hope to accomplish by sharing my thoughts in the meeting?

- If I did speak my mind, could it benefit my students or the school in general?

After answering these questions, you'll get a much clearer picture on why you are hesitant to speak up in a faculty meeting. Typically, we find that teachers are reluctant to speak up in meetings due to one of three things—personal insecurity, fear of being unpopular, or feelings of intimidation by a few others on the faculty.

So let's deal with each of those three. First, if you lack confidence and are therefore afraid to speak up, you're going to have to take the leap and do it anyway. You're a professional, and you deserve to have your professional voice heard. As long as what you are about to say is presented in a professional manner and it expresses your honest opinions about any given topic, you're going to be just fine. Take a deep breath and raise your hand. If you determine that your reluctance is due to a fear of being unpopular with other coworkers, remind yourself that you did not become a teacher to be popular with other teachers. You became a teacher to do whatever it takes to do what's best for your students, even if that's not always popular with everyone else. Have you ever noticed that the naysayers often get their way because they speak the loudest and the most often? The squeaky wheel gets the grease, as they say. Are you intimidated by some of your more negative coworkers? Many good teachers are. But it's important that you do what effective teachers do: don't allow your feelings of intimidation to stop you from acting in a way that benefits teaching and learning. If you do that, you lose, and, most important, the students lose.

DON'T FORGET

When you find yourself feeling reluctant to speak up in a faculty meeting, remember:

- You're a professional, and you have a right and an obligation to your students to share your thoughts, opinions, and ideas with your co-workers.

- The negative people will continue to take over discussions if you and other positive teachers remain silent.

- Always say what you have to say in the most positive, professional way possible. If others disagree, that's fine. Don't let it get to you.

- Don't just speak up for the sake of speaking up. But don't hold your tongue if you feel you can initiate any type of positive change.

- You did not become a teacher for the sake of appeasing your coworkers and their varied opinions. You became a teacher for the sake of the students. Be a voice of support for your students always.

- Even if you're new to the profession or new to the school, your opinions are valid and will be valued by other effective educators.

- If you're not popular with the negative teachers, congratulate yourself.

PART THREE

Classroom Management Challenges

26

YOU'RE STRUGGLING TO
GET ORGANIZED

IF THIS HAPPENS

Have you ever watched a TV show where professional organizers swoop in and turn a chaotic environment into neatness and organizational bliss? Have you found yourself wishing they would swoop in on your classroom? Why is there even a need for professional organizers? Why are there chains of stores that sell only organizational equipment and containers? And why are these stores so successful? Because life can be messy. So can classrooms.

To be an effective teacher, you have to remain organized. But that's not always easy. You start the year with a perfectly organized classroom—a classroom you worked in during the summer, getting everything neat, clean, and in place. And then it happens—the students arrive. Now you've got to keep them organized too. You have lesson plan folders and student folders and papers to grade and activity sheets to distribute and memos from the front office and notes from parents and record logs and computer files and lesson materials and on and on. If you don't stay on top of it, you are soon beneath it all, buried in a sea of chaos and disorganization. Is there really a way out?

TRY THIS

DOWNLOAD

Here are five simple tips for getting and staying organized in your classroom.

- Have a designated spot for everything. Papers to be returned to students have their own spot along with papers to be graded, project materials, materials for today's lessons, student supplies, paperwork to be turned in to the office, computer supplies, parent communications, folders for future lessons, student projects, and so forth. Label all of these, and don't allow anything to go where it doesn't belong. You know the saying, "A place for everything and everything in its place." If you don't have a place for everything, you're inviting chaos. Do the same with computer files. Make sure that they are in specific folders on your computer, organized, and easy to find without having to search your entire hard drive for a simple document.

- Keep a Today and Tomorrow box. It's a simple organizational tool that can save you time and headaches. For example, if you have a document that must be turned in to the office tomorrow, place it in the Tomorrow box. You might get to it today, but it's not necessary. If you have to answer a parent's note or e-mail, place it in the Today box. If you have a set of test papers that you want to return to your students today, place it in the Today box. You get the point. And simply be sure that the Today box is left empty at the end of the day. Then quickly put the contents of the Tomorrow box into the Today box so that it's ready for you when you arrive at school the following day.

- Explain the organization of the classroom to the students. Show them where certain things go and remind them often. Be clear on your expectations about how their desks or workstations should be kept. And hold them to it. When students are clear about your expectations, they're much more likely to comply.

- Allow the students to help you stay organized. Let's say you're working with a group of students and someone knocks on your door to deliver some paperwork that must be returned to the office by this afternoon. Simply ask a student to please place it in the Today box for you. Another way to get the students to help you is to provide about thirty seconds at the end of the class period for each student to clean his or her work area. This way, when the students leave there's no mess for you to clean.

- If you've let things go and you're overwhelmed and confused about where to even begin, ask an organized teacher for help. There are teachers who would *love* to help you if you'll only ask. These teachers are not likely to show up, uninvited, for an organization intervention.

DON'T FORGET

- Your classroom doesn't have to be perfectly neat in order to be well organized.
- Have a designated place for everything, and keep everything in its place.
- Students will learn from and mirror your model of—or lack of—organization in your classroom.
- Allow the students to take on some of the responsibility of keeping the classroom well organized.
- Today and Tomorrow boxes can serve well to keep you on top of your workload.
- Don't be too proud to ask for help if you need it.
- It's much less stressful and time-consuming to stay on top of organization than to dig yourself out of chaos.

27

YOUR CONTENT KNOWLEDGE IS SOLID, BUT YOUR MANAGEMENT SKILLS ARE LACKING

IF THIS HAPPENS

Nathan was a highly educated, intelligent teacher. His degrees and certifications, too numerous to list, spoke to his intellect. He wrote elaborate lesson plans for his high school physics classes, all of which were wasted due to his lack of management skills. He struggled through four years of teaching and finally resigned. His impressive understanding of physics was simply not enough to make him a successful teacher. Without management, very little learning was taking place in his classroom.

Barbara was a first-grade teacher. Her lesson plans were meticulous, and her content knowledge was sound. Her classroom, however, was chaotic. Students talked incessantly and roamed the classroom frequently. During learning activities, more students were off task than on task. Students blurted out answers or comments during discussions, and skirmishes between students were common. She begged and pleaded with them to pay attention, and she often resorted to using threats. She went home each day with a hoarse voice. Classroom management was lacking, and so was learning. Barbara quit her job after only two years of teaching.

One of the biggest challenges faced by teachers is classroom management. And one of the biggest mistakes teachers can make is attempting to teach the content before management is in place. Classroom management involves anything and everything a teacher does to ensure that the classroom runs smoothly—from establishing clear rules and procedures to arranging seating to planning activities that maximize student engagement. If classroom management is not in place, effective teaching and learning cannot occur.

The following are a few characteristics of classrooms lacking in management:

- Student talking unrelated to the lesson
- Students blurting out inappropriately
- Student confusion during assignments
- Students not following rules
- Lots of off-task behavior
- Lack of routines and procedures
- General chaos

TRY THIS

Do you recognize any of those characteristics in your own classroom? If so, there are simple steps that will help you take your classroom from chaotic to melodic:

- Know that recognizing and acknowledging a lack of management in your classroom is the first step to turning things around.

- Determine which areas of classroom management are most in need of improvement and address those first.

- Establish clear rules and expectations and share them with your students. Since rules regulate serious offenses and have consequences attached, limit them to a maximum of five.

- Establish one procedure for securing the attention of your students. Discuss it, practice it with the students, and use it consistently. (See Topic 28: Students Enter Your Class and Immediately Begin Talking.)

- Establish procedures for activities such as passing in papers, asking permission to speak, walking to or from the lunchroom, sharpening pencils, working in groups, working at computer stations, and so on. After much practice, these procedures will become routines.

- Remain consistent. Make your expectations clear so that students know what to do, when to do it, and how to do it.

- Plan learning activities that pique student interest and maximize engagement. If your rules and procedures are in place, you won't have to deal with chaos during these activities.

DON'T FORGET

The bottom line is that you cannot teach effectively without good classroom management. Though knowledge of content is important, it is not enough. You have to establish your management system before you can teach the content. Be clear on what it is you expect from your students, and once you establish your rules and procedures, adhere to them consistently.

Also remember that classroom management has at least as much to do with "class" as it does with "management." Making sure we behave in a professional manner every day goes a long way in ensuring positive behavior. And the most positive of all behaviors has to come from us.

28

STUDENTS ENTER YOUR CLASS AND IMMEDIATELY BEGIN TALKING

IF THIS HAPPENS

Do your students walk into your classroom quietly and get to work without your having to say a word? Are you laughing after reading that question? What typically happens when your students enter your classroom each day? Do they begin talking, and do you struggle to get them quiet and focused on learning tasks?

TRY THIS

Believe it or not, it is possible for your students to walk into class quietly and get to work immediately. You can do it, and so can any other teacher who follows these two simple steps:

- Establish a procedure for securing the attention of your students. For example, some teachers use a hand signal—maybe holding up five fingers. The students are taught that when the teacher uses this signal, they are to get quiet. It is often called Give Me Five, and it means "Stop and look at me." With this signal, the students also hold up five fingers. Other teachers use chimes or bells (even battery-operated doorbells). Some clap and say, "Clap once if you can hear me. Clap twice if you can hear me," and the students respond by clapping. The key is that you'll want to begin the year with this expectation. Trying to implement it later is much more difficult.

It really doesn't matter what your signal is or what the age of your students is. What matters is whether you use the signal consistently or inconsistently and whether you look happy or frustrated when using it. The winning combination is "consistent and happy." If you establish a procedure for getting students' attention, practice with the students, and then implement it consistently, looking pleasant every time, you'll experience success. The students will learn that this is what you do every time you need their attention. When they forget to follow a procedure on occasion, simply provide more practice. On the other hand, if you use the signal inconsistently and/or appear frustrated or upset when they don't follow it, it simply will not work. Again, it's not the signal itself that will help to secure student attention, but rather how you use it on a daily basis.

- Provide some type of daily warm-up activity (often referred to as "bell work") for the students to get busy on as soon as they enter the classroom. Make your bell work activities quick, fun, and relevant to the day's lesson. Post the bell work assignment in the same place every day so that students know where to look for it as soon as they are seated. Let's say that you are introducing a new topic today and would like to get a feel for your students' background knowledge. Your bell work might be: *Tell three things you know about _____ [and list the topic]. Be prepared to switch papers with your neighbor and compare what you both know when I give you the signal to do so.*

Bell work has advantages beyond engaging students as soon as they enter the room. It also provides you with time to take attendance, collect assignments, return graded assignments, and so on.

If you have a few students who begin talking during bell work, simply use your signal to get them back on task.

DON'T FORGET

Time on task is crucial to student achievement. You want your students actively engaged in learning activities from the moment they enter your classroom to the moment they leave. If students are accustomed to entering your classroom and visiting with their friends for the first few minutes of class, you'll have to spend some time retraining them. But if you establish your procedure for getting their attention, you can use it to get them started on their bell work. After they get accustomed to the routine of daily bell work, you should find yourself using your signal for attention less and less. Begin each class in a business-professional mode, and the students will adopt this same mindset.

> *What to remember about your procedure for getting students' attention:* be consistent with it and look happy while you're using it.

> *What to remember about bell work:* make each bell work assignment quick, fun, and relevant.

29

YOU HAVE A CHRONIC TALKER IN YOUR CLASS

IF THIS HAPPENS

Rather than asking if you've ever encountered a student who is a chronic talker, we will simply assume that you have. She's in every classroom, every year—the student who talks incessantly, who blurts out answers, who bothers other students with her chronic talking, and who can really test your patience. You've attempted to use numerous strategies to deter the behavior. You've learned that moving her seat doesn't help, because she will talk to *anyone*. Isolating her from other students only makes her talk to herself or talk louder so that her now-distant classmates can hear her. She's usually quite aware of how aggravating her behavior is, and she is aware that she tries your patience. Her behavior controls the behavior of others and possibly yours. That's powerful. She craves attention, even if it's negative. But take away her power, and the misbehavior will diminish drastically.

TRY THIS

Take the student aside, away from any other students (as you don't want to give her an audience) and speak kindly to her. Tell her you are concerned about the fact that she's having trouble remembering the procedure for talking. Tell her you know how awkward and embarrassing it can be to forget procedures in front of friends. Then tell her you will be happy to help her by giving her your free time either after class, during transition time, or at recess. (Notice that you are not taking away *her* time. Rather, you are giving her *your* time because you care.) When everyone else leaves the class, keep her with you and "practice" with her. Tell her to pretend she is in class and she has something she would like to say. Ask her to show you the correct procedure (raising her hand) for asking permission to speak. This takes less than a minute, so don't worry about losing too much of your own free time. Just find a minute, pull her aside, and practice. Tell her if she forgets the procedure again, you'll be happy to give her more practice time. Then send her on her way. If you can do this on *her* time, she will be much less likely to intrude on the time of others.

By doing this, you've accomplished several things: you've expressed caring and concern as opposed to aggravation, you've removed her audience, you've taken away the allure of a power struggle, and you've let her know that you will simply practice with her (as opposed to daring her to continue the misbehavior) when she "forgets." Prepare to be amazed. She won't understand what's happening, but you will.

From here forward, begin praising her when she is *not* talking out of turn. Turn the tables on her, and begin giving her more and more positive attention. Thank her for following the procedure for talking every time she follows it. When she does "forget" and speaks out of turn, simply ask, "What's the procedure?" If the problem ever gets chronic again, provide more practice. Do this always with a calm demeanor and a smile on your face.

DON'T FORGET

- When dealing with a chronic talker, be careful not to react negatively.
- Speak to the chronic talker out of concern and provide extra practice with her away from other students.

- When the chronic talker speaks out of turn, gently remind her about the procedure for asking permission to speak. Ask, "What's the procedure?" Do this with a smile on your face.

- Approach a chronic talker as though you think she is simply forgetting the procedure when she talks out of turn.

- Begin to praise the chronic talker as often as possible when she is not talking or when she is exhibiting any kind of positive behavior. She craves attention, so give it to her. But give her the positive kind.

30

YOUR STUDENTS MISBEHAVED WITH THE SUBSTITUTE TEACHER

IF THIS HAPPENS

You had to miss school unexpectedly. A substitute teacher was called in to take your place. You returned to school the next day to learn the following:

- Your students were less than well behaved with the substitute teacher.

- Some students were rude to the substitute teacher.

- Many students refused to do any work with the substitute teacher.

- Several students were sent to the principal by the substitute teacher.

- Students who normally behave well experienced "personality changes" with the substitute teacher.

- Very little, if any, of your lesson plan was actually used by the substitute teacher. (She was, after all, too busy trying to control the behavior of your students.)

You're upset with your students for behaving the way they did with the substitute teacher. You're embarrassed that your coworkers have undoubtedly heard about what happened in your classroom yesterday. (You know your principal heard, because he had to deal with the discipline referrals.) And you feel awful for the poor substitute teacher who had to endure the chaos in your classroom.

TRY THIS

Does this sound familiar? Many teachers will admit that they dread missing school for fear of what the students will or will not do in the care of a substitute teacher. But not *all* teachers dread having a substitute teacher take their place, because they've figured out a secret.

Here's what they do:

- First, they realize that human nature is human nature, and students will get away with exactly as much as they are allowed to get away with. Students will test anyone new if they are allowed to. So these teachers nip this in the bud very quickly.

- In the beginning of the school year, they train the students with "procedures for substitute teacher days." These procedures include assigning jobs to every student in the class. For instance, one person is the greeter. He greets the substitute teacher. Another student shows the substitute teacher where things are in the classroom—the lesson plans, supplies, and so on. Another student explains the regular teacher's procedure for getting students' attention. Another passes out papers. And on and on until everyone has some type of responsibility for helping the substitute teacher feel welcome and for familiarizing the substitute teacher with the general workings of the class. Every student has the job of thanking the substitute teacher on the way out of the room at the end of class. You get the idea. (This can be used effectively at any grade level. Obviously, you will need to make it apply to your personal setting, adapting it to the appropriate age levels of your students.)

- Once jobs are assigned and the substitute-teacher-day procedures are established, the teacher practices with the students. On occasion, the teacher says, "We'll pretend that I am a substitute teacher today. Assume your roles." Students love these drills, and it gives them the opportunity to practice so that they know exactly what to do when it is an actuality, not a drill.

So now, when you are absent, the students feel responsible and important, as opposed to feeling as if they have just been freed from their leashes!

If you don't believe this works, then you've never tried it. And this technique is not reserved for elementary classrooms. We continue to work with teachers at all grade levels who use it successfully. As an added bonus, the substitute teachers are overwhelmed by the responsible nature and good behavior of your students. They ask to return to your room any time.

DON'T FORGET

There are three basic points to remember regarding leaving your students in the care of a substitute teacher:

- Students will succumb to human nature and be tempted to behave less than appropriately with a substitute teacher. Know this in advance.

- You can nip this inevitable problem in the bud by training your students in exactly what to do when you are absent. Delegate responsibilities to each so that they feel empowered in your absence—empowered to be of assistance as opposed to being a nuisance.

- Practice the "substitute drill" on occasion to ensure that students remain abreast of exactly what to do in the event of your absence. Remember that when students are clear on what is expected of them, they are much more likely to *do* what is expected of them.

Though nothing works perfectly every time, and we can't guarantee that every student will behave perfectly even in your presence, much less in the presence of a substitute teacher, rest assured that being prepared and having a plan for substitutes beats not having a plan every time. Remember, too, that a substitute teacher should not introduce new content. You're likely going to have to reteach it anyway. But make sure that students have plenty of meaningful tasks to accomplish. Free time with a substitute teacher never goes well.

31

A PARTICULAR STUDENT IS PUSHING YOUR BUTTONS

IF THIS HAPPENS

Desiree is this year's challenge. It seems that a version of her is in every class, every year. She's the student who has figured out how to push your buttons—every last one of them. You're losing your patience, and you're running out of ideas to try to squelch this frustrating behavior. If you say "stop," she says "go." If you say "up," she says "down." She knows how to make the veins protrude in your neck. She seems to thrive on making you feel exasperated. She also enjoys the fact that her classmates know that she, a student, is powerful enough to control you, an adult.

Have you heard other teachers using the old saying, "It only takes one"? Well, it actually does only take one—one teacher. It takes one teacher to react to a student's antics, and off they go—to a power struggle. Power struggles, of course, are futile. And button pushing, for some students, is downright fun.

So you realize that Desiree has succeeded in her quest to "get you." This has now become a game for her, and she has no intentions of stopping. In fact, she's becoming ever more clever in her attempts to make you lose your patience. So now it's your turn to turn it completely around. If you do it correctly, Desiree will have no idea what's happening. You can accomplish this by using some, or all, of the following tips.

TRY THIS

Here are a few simple tips for hiding your buttons from your students:

- First and foremost, make a commitment to hide *all* of your buttons, starting today, from the students.

- Know in advance what types of behavior push your buttons. And know in advance how you will take extra care to hide those buttons—every one of them—from your students.

- Have a plan in place so that you won't be caught off guard. "The next time Desiree (or another student) does _____, I will simply _____." And follow through consistently with that plan.

- Avoid acting on impulse. You'll usually regret it. That's why you should plan what to say beforehand. And if a student still catches you off guard in a way you had not planned, step back and think before you act.

- Control your words. And don't speak your words immediately. Silence truly is golden when someone is trying to get you to react.

- Control your body language. Even if you don't say anything, if you clench your teeth or stare up at the ceiling or appear aggravated in any way, you've lost.

- Decide in advance that you will not let that particular student know when she is upsetting you. This doesn't mean that you should not deal with a misbehaving student. Rather, you should deal with the student calmly—maintaining your cool, at least on the outside.

- Speak with her privately. Attach consequences to her actions if necessary, but let her know in advance it is a choice she's making. Act as though it doesn't bother you—it's her choice.

- Ignore what can be ignored.

- Give the offending student some power, but not the kind she is seeking. Instead, praise her when she is behaving well, and start to give her small doses of responsibility, setting up more reasons to praise her and shift the focus off of her typically negative behavior.

DON'T FORGET

The only way a student can have power over you is if you allow her to. Though not always easy, it is imperative that you take every precaution to ensure that your students no longer know you even *have* buttons that can be pushed. Teachers who "have no buttons" deal with far fewer discipline problems. When faced with discipline challenges from students, they deal with these challenges calmly, professionally, and away from the watchful eyes of the rest of their students. They flat out refuse to allow their emotions to be controlled by their students. And they do this with smiles on their faces, even though they're sometimes using one of the most effective tricks of all effective teachers: faking it.

32

STUDENTS HAVE A PROBLEM WITH "TELLING ON OTHERS"

IF THIS HAPPENS

If you think that "telling on others" is reserved for elementary-age students, think again. Every year, it doesn't take long to spot the ones who can't wait to "tell on the others." (Whether the word of the day is snitching, narcing, ratting, or tattling, students of all ages tend to do it.) We won't get into the whys. Instead we'll acknowledge the fact that self-appointed "informants" are in every classroom, and we'll share some tricks for alleviating the problem.

First, be clear on what "telling on others" is and is not, at least for the purpose of the classroom. Though by definition *tattling* means to tell about another's wrongdoings, we don't consider it to be tattling when a student tells a teacher that one student is bullying another student. We do, however, consider it to be tattling when a student reports that Thomas is picking his nose. Tattling in the classroom carries a negative connotation—it has no real purpose, and it really doesn't help anyone involved. Telling of a serious wrongdoing, however, can lead to positive results.

As we all know, there are some students who can't wait to report on the others—so-and-so made an ugly gesture, so-and-so said a bad word, so-and-so stayed home today but isn't really sick, and the like. These behaviors, of course, need to be curtailed and ultimately eliminated. On the other side of that, behaviors that stop others from being harmed need to be encouraged.

TRY THIS

The following are four easy steps to help curtail the behavior of students who tell on others:

Step 1. Teach your students the difference between "ratting someone out" and reporting a serious issue. We often assume they know the difference, and typically they don't. Provide age-appropriate examples and help them to determine which examples represent "ratting someone out" and which do not. When necessary, provide refresher lessons.

Step 2. Tell the students you will help them to remember the difference between the two (when they forget—and some *will* forget) by saying a key phrase such as "Think about that one first." That will be your non-confrontational way of having the student question whether what he is telling you affects his or another's health or life in a serious way. Soon the students (the chronic tattlers) actually begin thinking about it before you have to remind them to do so.

Step 3. Don't allow it. Make it very clear from day one that telling on others (for the simple sake of telling on others) is not something you allow or encourage in any way. And then continue to nip it in the bud each time it happens by using your key phrase. Occasionally, you may need to speak to a chronic tattler in private and provide some remediation regarding what's appropriate to tell about others and what's not.

Step 4. Don't respond with emotion. Ignoring or making sure that you never overreact to a student telling on another will often get the student to stop the behavior.

DON'T FORGET

Chronic informants learn very quickly which teachers support and enable this bad habit and which do not. If the habit is fed, it will grow. If it is starved, it will fade away. It's really that simple.

33

A STUDENT BRINGS AN ISSUE FROM OUTSIDE INTO THE CLASSROOM

IF THIS HAPPENS

Ms. Combative was standing at her door as the students arrived. She noticed that Phillip was in an exceptionally bad mood, angrily talking to a classmate about something that had just happened outside during transition time. Ms. Combative did what Ms. Combative does—she readied herself for battle. Before Phillip had a chance to walk into the classroom, Ms. Combative said, "Whatever happened outside will stay outside! Do you understand?" Phillip defensively tried to explain why he was so upset. Ms. Combative stopped him in midsentence. "Leave it outside, I said!" Phillip stormed into the classroom and slammed his books onto his desk, mumbling to himself. Ms. Combative warned him again, and an argument ensued. Phillip soon landed in the principal's office. When he returned to class, he was even angrier, and a bad situation only became worse. Situation fueled, conflict escalated, and no solution in sight.

Ms. Preemptive was standing at her door as the students arrived. She noticed that Phillip was in an exceptionally bad mood, angrily talking to a classmate about something that had just happened outside during transition time. Ms. Preemptive did what Ms. Preemptive does—she readied herself for problem solving. Before Phillip had a chance to walk into the classroom,

Ms. Preemptive said, "I can tell you're upset about something, and I want to help if I can. Would you mind just taking a seat for a minute as I get everyone busy? Then we can talk. Thanks so much." Phillip quietly went to his desk and took a seat. As promised, Ms. Preemptive got everyone busy and then stepped outside the door with Phillip. They discussed what had happened. It was a legitimate issue, and Phillip was justifiably upset. He had witnessed someone picking on his younger sister. Ms. Preemptive promised Phillip she would look into the matter. She told him she admired the fact that he was protective of his sister, and she said she completely understood why he had gotten so upset. She also told him how much she appreciated the fact that he had not taken matters into his own hands, but instead had taken the issue to her, an adult. This, she said, was the most mature way he could have handled the situation.

The entire conversation took less than two minutes. Both Phillip and Ms. Preemptive walked back into the classroom calmly. Situation defused, conflict avoided, and solution in sight.

TRY THIS

It's obvious that you'll want to try Ms. Preemptive's approach and avoid any approach similar to that of Ms. Combative. When a student is upset, your first goal is to try to help him calm down enough to discuss what is upsetting him. Once you know that, you can help him to resolve the issue. This way, you're attacking a problem, not a person. The person on the other end of that problem needs to know you are on his side and willing to help him. Once he knows that, he will more likely trust you to provide that needed assistance. Ms. Preemptive did just that: she calmly addressed the fact that Phillip was upset, she told him she wanted to help, she gave him time to catch his breath and calm down a bit, and then she had a discussion with him that led to a solution.

Everything Ms. Combative did was ineffective, because it was confrontational. Teachers are supposed to help students, not do battle with them.

DON'T FORGET

You can't change the fact that students occasionally come to class upset about things that have happened outside of your classroom. You can, however, control your reaction to the student and help the student deal with whatever it is that is bothering him before what's bothering him becomes a bother to others.

Defuse, don't react, and use the fact that a calm approach, instead of a reproach, will yield a better outcome than will coming undone.

34

CLASSROOM DISCUSSIONS GO OFF IN A DIFFERENT DIRECTION

IF THIS HAPPENS

The focus of the current chapter you and the class are discussing is wild animals. The discussion leads to determining how wild animals differ from domesticated animals. Someone mentions that a cheetah is a member of the cat family, but it is quite different from a domesticated cat. Soon students are sharing their stories about whose cat has the most creative name, whose cat died recently, where and how their cats were buried, who has the most cats, whose cats fight with dogs, whose dog died recently, who prefers cats to dogs, who prefers snakes to mice, who enjoyed the movie *Catwoman*, whether there should be a sequel, whether there should ever be a *Dogwoman* character, the technology involved in making animated characters come to life on the screen, and so on.

It happens so quickly, you hardly see it coming. And it's not the first time. Now you're thinking, "They know exactly what they're doing. They're trying to get me off task. I am not going to let them do this to me yet again. They're always trying to outsmart me. Are they really smarter than I am? Would I make a good *Catwoman*? Hey—wait a minute." You suddenly appear flustered and you let the students know it. You say something like,

"That is completely off topic, and you all know it. Now let's get back on track."

The students now know that, whether they meant to or not, they managed yet again to control your emotions. And remember: that's the last thing you ever want your students to do—be in control of your emotions. Oops.

TRY THIS

The following are tips for keeping students focused on the topic of discussion, along with ways to get them back when they stray:

- Realize that sometimes students—at all ages and grade levels—will consciously try to get you off topic. If that is the case, act oblivious to the fact that you are aware of their motives. Simply say, "I'd love to hear about your *Catwoman* collection. Remind me about it again as soon as the bell rings. We'll discuss it then. Thanks." By the way, they rarely stay after class to share their story. But if they do, simply listen to it as though it's the most interesting story you've ever heard. Remember that we want to use *their* time, not *class* time.

- Realize that sometimes students stray from the topic without realizing it. They really were not trying to "get you." They simply got off topic. As smoothly and calmly as possible, steer them back to the topic.

- Don't take it personally. Even if you know beyond doubt that your students were trying to get you off topic intentionally, do not take their actions personally. Simply steer them back to the topic of discussion.

- Let them know you're interested in what they have to say by saying something like, "I'd love to hear the names of all of your pets, but we don't have time right now. I'll make it a part of our creative writing assignment later if you remind me. Thanks."

- Redirect them by "faking them out." When a student mentions that his cat fights with his dog, say, "Oh, I'm glad you brought that up. Did you know that wild animals fight with other animals also? Now, since we are discussing cheetahs right now, let's do a quick online search to find out which animals cheetahs will and won't fight with."

- Remember most importantly that *you* control the class discussions—not the students. Just do so calmly, and never let on that you think they may be "up to something."

DON'T FORGET

Keeping students on topic is a management skill. With practice, you'll be able to keep your students focused on the topic of discussion—and you'll be able to do this in a calm, seemingly effortless manner. The key is to recognize when it begins to happen and take quick action to redirect them. But avoid at all costs letting your emotions show if in fact their actions annoy you in any way. Showing your true feelings will only entice them to do it more. Use psychology and act as though you didn't even notice that they were off topic and, with clever questioning, steer them right back to where you want them to be.

35

YOUR CLASSROOM NEEDS A MAKEOVER, BUT YOU'RE JUST NOT A DECORATOR

IF THIS HAPPENS

Is your classroom suffering from a case of the blahs? Does it lack color? Does it possibly lack organization? And does it lack style? Does it feel cozy and welcoming, or does it feel cold? Could your classroom use a makeover?

You're probably already thinking, "Okay, my classroom could use a makeover, but I'm not a decorator. I wouldn't even know where to begin. Plus, makeovers cost money. I'm a teacher. I have no extra money!"

The good news is that classrooms can be made over quickly and with very little money. Sometimes, by using items you already have and just sprucing things up or arranging them differently, you can add style and pizzazz to your classroom. Simple, inexpensive changes can turn a dull, mundane-looking classroom into a colorful, inviting learning environment.

TRY THIS

DOWNLOAD

Here are a few simple tips for a quick classroom makeover:

- Almost every classroom has a resident artist or two. You know who they are. Enlist their help. Have them paint a mural on a section of wall or allow them to jazz up your bulletin boards with their expertise. If by some chance your own class does not have an artist, ask the art teacher to recommend the most skilled students in the school. They'll jump at the chance to show off their craft.

- There are teachers on every faculty who love to decorate and who are skilled at decorating. You'll flatter them if you ask for their expert advice, and they are almost always happy to lend a helping hand. Ask!

- Do a quick Internet search for classroom makeover images. You'll get more ideas than you can possibly use. Ask your teaching buddies on social media to share images of their own classrooms with you. They'll be flattered.

- Have your students help you get things picked up and organized so that there are designated places and spaces for everything.

- You don't have to paint in order to add color.

- Designate several different areas in your classroom—areas for sitting and reading, areas for computer use, areas for working on projects, and so forth.

- Take a simple piece of scrap carpet or a small area rug, add a few chairs and maybe a table, and you've got a reading corner or a workstation.

- Bring a plant or two into the room to add color. Allow the students to care for the plants; they love doing this.

- Display student work in order to add interest and color to a wall or a bulletin board.

- A few colorful storage containers can add style to a classroom.

- If you're looking for a certain item, like a beanbag chair, don't go out and buy one. Ask the students if anyone has one to give away or to lend to the class for the school year. If you send a note home to parents telling them your room is in need of certain items, you'll be surprised to see what they will gladly lend or donate.

- Take an old bookshelf and add a colorful coat of paint to it.
- If you're still in need of a few items, your local thrift store can be a treasure trove.
- Turn a couple of parents loose. There are always home decorating TV show fans in search of a blank canvas.

DON'T FORGET

By enlisting the support of a few students and a creative coworker or two, your classroom can experience an amazing transformation in no time at all. Remember: nothing fancy, nothing expensive, and nothing time-consuming. You're busy enough. But you're also dedicated enough to know the importance of providing a colorful, learning-friendly, welcoming environment for your students. So don't be too proud to ask for help. And don't be surprised if you don't even recognize your classroom in a day or two.

PART FOUR

Instructional Challenges

36

YOU TEND TO TEACH THE WAY YOU WERE TAUGHT

IF THIS HAPPENS

So you grew up in the "good ole days." Students did what their teachers asked them to do. Classrooms were quiet places. Teachers taught to the whole class in basically the same way. Neat desks were in neat rows. Lessons were introduced on Mondays and wrapped up on Fridays. There were no special accommodations for anyone. Students either got it or they didn't. The old lecture—read the chapter—answer the questions at the end of the chapter—complete the worksheet—review—and test was the method of choice for many. It was all so neat, so simple, so stress-free. And oh, the evils of technology. Educators engaged in long-running arguments about whether or not to allow students to use calculators in the classroom. If we allowed them that crutch, we would ruin them. Remember?

And here you are today, in a world that only remotely resembles the one in which you grew up. Research has come very far in helping us understand how the brain learns best. It has made many of yesterday's teaching techniques seem almost silly—at least in today's world. Teaching techniques have changed drastically. Technology is developing so rapidly, it's impossible to keep up.

You occasionally find yourself yearning for the "good ole days." You've even heard yourself defending the teaching techniques of yesteryear, saying, "That's the way I learned it, and it worked for me." You often find yourself teaching mostly in ways that your teachers taught you. And you're not alone. Many of your coworkers are doing the same—*many* of them.

Why is it that so many teachers tend to teach the way they were taught? And is that necessarily a bad thing? Well, that depends. There are tried-and-true techniques that work as well today as they did many years ago. There are others that do not. Let's face it—we are creatures of habit.

Here are a few of the more common reasons many teachers teach the way they were taught:

- It's what they know. They saw it, they lived it, and so they can relate to it. Teaching in a familiar way becomes a habit, and habits are difficult to break.
- It's easier. Teaching everyone in the same way is far easier than accommodating a wide variety of learner differences.
- Learning new techniques pushes teachers out of their comfort zones. It can be downright scary.

If you find yourself teaching the way you were taught because of any of the aforementioned reasons, don't beat yourself up. You're human. But do challenge yourself to consider that there may be more effective methods today that work better with today's learners.

TRY THIS

First, be brutally honest with yourself. Do you ever teach the way you were taught? If so, why? The answer to that question will provide valuable information. Is it that you're doing what effective teachers do, using many innovative teaching techniques while still incorporating techniques of the past that continue to prove successful today? If so, you're on target. If you're using methods of the past because those methods are familiar and comfortable, you may want to rethink your current approach. But don't be afraid or allow yourself to feel overwhelmed. You cannot be expected to go out tomorrow and change everything you are doing; nor should you.

Small steps can lead to big changes. Try taking the following small steps in order to update your teaching methods and improve your effectiveness:

- Ask a trusted coworker for tips. No two teachers are alike. There's a wealth of resources on any faculty—resources that often go untapped. Effective teachers are constantly "begging, borrowing, and stealing" from their coworkers.

- Befriend a new teacher. You can both learn from each other. Teachers right out of college often bring fresh ideas and techniques along with them. And these new teachers are hungry to drink in your wisdom and knowledge. A true win-win.

- Do a quick Internet search on how to teach the topic you're teaching, and you will find more ideas than you can imagine. Don't read it all. Just search for a few minutes until you find something that seems doable for you and your students. Don't throw out your plans; just tweak them.

- Make it a habit to try one new technique every day. Just one. Don't be surprised if you soon find yourself abandoning many of your older methods. And don't be surprised if you find yourself holding on to a few of those older methods, too.

- Learn from your students. Ask about new things they'd like to try or ask them how they like to learn best. Though students don't always know what's best for them, they often do have wonderful ideas for helping us to help them.

- Do a quick "Who's doing the talking?" assessment. If you realize that you do most of the talking and that your students are usually expected to be silent, rethink it. Today's classrooms should be social and highly interactive. There should be at least as much student talk as teacher talk.

- Don't fight technology—*embrace* it. And begin to incorporate a little (and then a lot) more of it into your teaching. The students love using it, don't they?

- Use social media to draw ideas from peers outside of your school.

DON'T FORGET

- Teaching the way you were taught simply because it's the way you were taught is not sound practice.

- Old habits die hard. So don't be too hard on yourself or place unreasonable demands on yourself. Try one new technique a day. That's more than doable.

- Find someone who teaches the same content or grade level as you and ask for new ideas. You won't appear ineffective; on the contrary, you'll appear cutting edge.

- Some of what worked well in the past still works well today, but not all of it.

- Teach for the present and the future, not the past. Today's students live in today's world, and we're preparing them for *their futures*, not *our pasts*.

37

YOU'RE OVERWHELMED BY NEW TECHNOLOGY

IF THIS HAPPENS

Do you ever find yourself feeling overwhelmed by today's technology? Like you just can't keep up? Does it seem that by the time you learn to use a new device, that device is already obsolete and it's time to learn to use the newer technology that just replaced it? And do you often feel as though your students are more technologically savvy than you are? In today's world, many children can use smartphones before they can dress themselves!

If you find yourself feeling a little overwhelmed, you're not alone. Researchers are already studying the fact that many of us are feeling overwrought in the face of so many technological advancements.

There's no arguing that technology is beginning to change the way we teach and the way our students learn. Technology has opened a whole new world to us and to our students. Therefore, gone are the days of burying our heads in the sand, hoping technology will somehow go away.

Technology is not inherently good or bad. Rather our use (or misuse) of it makes it so. If you find yourself feeling like you just can't keep up, relax. First, know that you're not alone, and second, know that you don't have to be the most technologically literate person on the faculty to be the best teacher in the school. You can't, however, continue to be a great teacher if you ignore significant advancements in teaching, learning, and technology.

Consider Jack's experience. He was a self-proclaimed technology geek. He owned the latest devices, knew how to use all the latest programs and operating systems, and could build his own computers. However, he lacked interpersonal skills and was never able to connect with the students. He quit teaching after only six months. So please realize that we are not suggesting that being technologically savvy is enough on its own to make you an effective teacher.

Your good old tried-and-true teaching skills are just as important as they ever were. But also realize that you can't rely solely on what you used to do even a few years ago. The times are changing, and you have to adapt and change with them.

TRY THIS

Here are a few suggestions for maintaining a healthy perspective in an ever-changing, technologically advanced world:

- Don't try to stay on top of everything. You can't. But *do* try to learn about new technology that affects you in the classroom. Designate maybe an hour or two a week to learn something new.

- Find out first what your school expects of you. (Maybe there's a new computer program or app your school expects you to use.) Learn to do what is expected first, and then augment your teaching with your own technology or your own ideas later.

- If students know more than you about a particular device, program, or other tool, then by all means allow them to teach you.

- Enlist the support of a technologically literate person on your faculty and ask for help.

- Experiment with new technology, but be patient. Allow yourself to make mistakes. When you feel confused, intimidated, or overwhelmed, ask for help. We're all learning together.

- Don't use technology just for the sake of using it. Use technology in a way that enhances your lessons and your students' learning.

DON'T FORGET

Today's teachers are using technology to be more efficient, more effective, more connected, and to enhance the learning opportunities of their students. As long as you are moving forward and continually learning something new, you'll be just fine. You can't possibly be up-to-date on all the latest advancements. No one can. But it is important to keep abreast of certain changes in technology that affect teaching and learning. However, be careful not to let the changing times and technology overtake and overwhelm you. Everything in moderation.

38

MANY STUDENTS PERFORMED POORLY ON A TEST

IF THIS HAPPENS

A middle school teacher was speaking with two coworkers after school one day. She said, "I don't know what happened. I gave my students a test Wednesday, and many of them failed it. Even the ones who passed did not do well. Is it me?" Her two coworkers were quick to offer their opinions, both quite different.

> **Coworker A:** If a lot of them failed, then just curve the grades. That's what I do.

> **Coworker B:** Well, if they all did poorly, it might simply mean they weren't ready to be tested on that material yet. When this happens to me, I always look to myself and my teaching first.

There are a variety of reasons that students perform poorly on tests. But when most perform poorly, it can be a red flag telling us we did not fully prepare them and we tested them too soon.

TRY THIS

If you ever give a test on which most of your students perform poorly, always look to yourself first. If you take the advice of coworker A and simply curve the grades, you've succeeded in possibly appeasing the students by giving them higher grades. But if they don't understand the material, you still have to reteach and then retest.

When many students do not succeed on a particular test, determine the following:

1. Did I teach the material thoroughly?

2. Did my informal assessments (prior to the test) give me any inclination that my students were not ready to be tested? Did I actually provide any kind of informal assessment?

3. Did I provide enough practice time for students to master the skills before they were formally tested?

4. Was the format of the test consistent with the way that I taught the material?

Your answers to these questions will provide valuable information. Often, we realize that the format of the test was simply unfamiliar to the students. The test results were, in actuality, not indicative of the students' understanding. For instance, an elementary teacher shared the following:

I give my students a spelling test every week. On every spelling test, there are fifteen words to spell. We discuss the words all week, we practice spelling them and using them in sentences, and they know exactly which words will be on the test. There are no surprises. They typically do well on their spelling tests. This week, more than half of my class failed the test. But I soon realized that it was my fault. Instead of giving them a page numbered 1–15 and then calling out the words for them to spell, I changed the format. For each word, I gave four choices, only one of which was spelled correctly. They had to choose the one that was spelled correctly and circle it. I actually thought it would be an "easy" test, given that the correctly spelled word was already on the page. I had no idea how confusing this format would be to them. So I quickly threw out those tests because the scores were only an indication of their confusion. That doesn't mean I won't test that way again, but in the future, I'll teach that way before I test that way.

As any teacher knows, not all students do well on every test. If only a few students do poorly on a test, you should not blame yourself. You will, however, want to provide some remediation, but only to those few. But when most students do poorly, it usually signifies that either the students were not ready to be tested or that the testing format was incongruent with the teaching format (See Topic 40: You're Unsure How to Write a Good Test).

DON'T FORGET

- When many students perform poorly on a test, determine why.
- Resist the temptation to simply curve the grades when students don't do well on a test. If they don't understand the material, you still have to reteach and retest.
- Provide plenty of opportunities for students to practice the skills on which they will be tested.
- Provide ongoing, informal assessments while teaching in order to determine when students are ready to be tested formally.
- Test material in the same way that you have taught the material.

39

YOU'RE CONFUSED ABOUT ASSIGNING HOMEWORK

IF THIS HAPPENS

Homework: a dirty word to most students, a dreaded word for many parents, and often a confusing word for teachers. Teachers struggle with how much homework they should assign, what types of homework they should assign, how they can get their students to actually *do* the homework, and whether it's even beneficial. If you look into research on homework, you will find conflicting conclusions. Some swear by it, and others swear against it. But most will agree that students should not be overloaded with it. And no one really knows the magic number of minutes students should spend doing homework after school each day. What we do know, however, is that overloading students with too much homework leads to many students simply refusing to do it. Others do it, but it involves a daily struggle with their parents. Some don't understand the assignments, leaving them feeling frustrated and inadequate. And yes, some students breeze right through it. That doesn't mean they enjoy it. In fact, students who already understand a concept often resent having to do more of what they already know how to do.

In an attempt to clarify some of the confusion, let's look at the real purpose of homework. The real purpose of homework should be to provide more practice for what has already been learned in the classroom. It stands to reason that practicing a new skill helps to promote improvement and, ultimately, mastery. So a legitimate reason to assign homework is for the purpose of practicing skills the students are learning in class. You, the teacher, are hoping that the students will return tomorrow a little more adept at a new skill than they were when they left your class today.

So where have we gone wrong? We've missed the boat when we assign homework that is too time-consuming, when assignments are confusing to students, when assignments require students to teach themselves something that has not been taught at all or at least not taught thoroughly, and when students don't see the assignment as relevant. Consider that if a student doesn't understand a concept and begins practicing a skill incorrectly, we then have to undo the damage when he returns to school. All of these reasons provide insight into why homework has become a dreaded word.

So how do you know if the homework you're assigning is appropriate and beneficial?

TRY THIS

The following should be considered when assigning homework: Does the assignment serve to provide more practice for what has been taught in class? Is the assignment quick, relevant, and doable? Will you *use* the homework results to provide remediation to students who don't understand, to provide enrichment to those who do, and to guide your teaching? Is homework affecting student grades? A word of caution about this one: student grades in a particular subject should reflect their knowledge and skills based on evaluations. Can they perform this skill or not when they are tested? Yet some students receive failing grades for not turning in homework, which in turn affects their final grade in that subject. In such a case, the final grade is not an accurate representation of what the student knows and can do. It has been tainted by the fact that he failed to turn in a homework assignment or two.

When assigning homework, also consider that some students are receiving homework from several other teachers. Always assume that your assignment is not their only assignment. If you are the students' only teacher, just take care not to assign too much homework in too many subjects. Pick and choose what you feel is most important for your students to go home and practice. And make sure that that practice time is minimal. Kids need time to be kids.

Each time you are considering assigning homework, ask yourself, What is the purpose of this assignment? The answer to that question will help you determine what to assign and whether to assign it at all.

DON'T FORGET

- Homework should be for the purpose of practicing what has been learned in class.

- Homework should be seen by students as quick, attainable, and meaningful.

- Please be cautious about allowing homework to affect a student's final grade, because the final grade should represent what the student knows and can do, not how many homework assignments he missed or how he scored while he was practicing.

- Some teachers choose to assign a consequence for students failing to turn in homework assignments. That is the teacher's choice. But it's not the same thing as allowing the missed assignment to affect the student's final grade.

- Keep homework to a minimum. And don't assign it every day. Remember that students spend long hours each day at school. They deserve some time to themselves.

40

YOU'RE UNSURE HOW TO WRITE A GOOD TEST

IF THIS HAPPENS

Consider that you are teaching simple addition to your students. They are adding one-digit numbers. You teach it all week, and they seem to be grasping the concept. They go home each night with twenty addition problems for practice. In class, you provide lots of practice. They count various other objects in the room all week long. If you put two apples on a student's desk and add another to it, she can tell you that the total number of apples on her desk is three. She gets it! When she sees $1 + 2 = \_\_$, she can correctly answer 3. Then you say, "Sally has one apple. Tim gives her two of his. How many apples does Sally now have?" Don't be at all surprised if the student cannot answer this question. She has never had to solve an addition problem presented in the form of a word problem before, using reasoning to turn the word problem into $1 + 2 = 3$. She will very likely feel confused and overwhelmed. But it doesn't mean that she can't add one-digit numbers. She is simply confused by the context in which the problem is presented because it is new and unfamiliar to her. In order to test her in this way, you must first teach her in this way.

Imagine that you are a basketball coach. You are teaching your players to do a lay-up. You model the technique necessary to execute this type of shot, you teach it, you discuss it, and you practice it with them. Then you allow the players to practice on their own as you give feedback. You do this all week long. Now it's time for the test. What's the best way to test them? The best way to test them is to have them demonstrate the technique for executing this type of shot. Would it make sense to give them a multiple-choice or true-or-false test on lay-ups? Would any kind of written test be appropriate? Even if a player could pass a written test, does it mean she can execute a lay-up in a game of basketball? And isn't it possible that a player who is quite adept at this skill might perform poorly on a written test about lay-ups? But this is what we sometimes do to students in the classroom. We test them in ways that are different from how we have taught them. Or we judge their ability according to a test that does not require that they actually demonstrate the ability. We teach things like grammar lessons, and then we ask them to spit back grammar rules on a test. But even if a student can memorize rules, it does not tell us whether he can *use* those rules in his writing. So how do you know if you're testing students appropriately?

TRY THIS

The following are tips for writing effective tests:

- Begin with the end in mind. Know what you will test before you start teaching. In other words, be clear on your objectives for every lesson you teach. Know exactly what you want students to know or be able to do following the lesson or the unit.

- Tell the students at the beginning of each lesson exactly what they will be learning and how they will be tested. As you teach, you should be assessing their understanding informally through your observations, through their work samples, and through your questioning. When you teach this way, you will know when students are or are not ready to be tested.

- Be careful when constructing tests about test items that are confusing. The results from multiple-choice questions usually tell you very little about what a student knows or can do. They're easy to write and even easier to grade, but they can be very confusing to students. If you do include multiple-choice items, avoid choices such as "all of the above" and "none of the above," because these can lead to "confusion for all."

- Construct your test items so that students have to explain or demonstrate what they have learned. But make sure they have had practice doing this *before* they are formally tested on it.

- Remember that much test anxiety is alleviated when students are clear on what they are learning, how well they are performing, and how they will be tested on their knowledge or skills.

- Do not add surprise items on tests. And be careful to grade only what you are testing. For instance, a student should not receive a poor grade on a science test because of poor grammar or spelling. It's not that grammar and spelling are unimportant, but this was not a grammar or spelling test. Feel free to correct grammar and spelling, but don't base the grade on it.

DON'T FORGET

Know your objectives, make sure the students know the objectives, give them feedback on how they are doing, and test them that way. No surprises. That's not to say that you don't make a test challenging. But challenging is different from confusing or impossible. Students should always be clear about what material they will be tested on and how they will be tested on it.

41

YOU TEACH MANY STUDENTS AT MANY DIFFERENT LEVELS

IF THIS HAPPENS

Your students enter your classroom on the very first day of school—all twenty-eight of them, at least for this class period. Your job is to motivate them, inspire them, and teach them a fairly specific set of skills and information by the end of the year. You soon realize that there are vast differences in their ability levels, their interests, their experiences, and their behaviors. Yet that doesn't change the fact that you are expected to help them all reach their full potential. Difficult? Yes. But as any teacher knows, there is no such thing as having even two students who are at exactly the same level. Even identical twins are never *truly* identical. Yet here you are, with a classroom of students from different parents and different backgrounds, with different ability levels, interests, and experiences. And you are determined to reach and teach them all so that each will learn and succeed. How can you possibly do it?

Today, the term is *differentiated instruction*—otherwise known as highly effective teaching—which encompasses identifying what students know, what they want to know, what interests them, and how they learn best, and then teaching them what they need to know in a way that they will best be able to learn it. In other words, we adjust to them—we *teach the way they learn* as opposed to *expecting them to learn the way we teach*.

Though we could write an entire book on this topic, we will address it succinctly here by using a simple analogy. Think of your classroom as a swimming pool. You're the instructor and you're teaching a group of six-year-olds to swim. That's the goal—to teach them to swim so that they can survive in water. On the very first day, you will see that no two of your students will be at exactly the same level. Some will swim quite well, meaning they would not drown if you threw them into the deep water. Others might survive if you threw them in, because they do have some skills. Others would definitely drown. But even those who could stay afloat should not be trusted to go off on their own into the deep end of the pool just yet. Still, that group would be bored if you talked to them about how to hold your breath so as to not swallow water. But a few need this skill in order to move forward.

So you start off with letting them *show* you what they *know*. You lead a discussion about their experiences and you learn quite a lot from that. You let them demonstrate what they can do—all in the shallow end, of course. You lead a discussion on water safety that includes everyone. And then you get one group (and sometimes a group is two or three students) busy practicing a particular stroke or a more advanced breathing technique. Another group might be practicing a more basic breathing technique. And yet another group will be with you as you show them how to hold their breath and quickly put their faces in the water. You're watching all three, and you go to each group, providing guidance, assessing, answering questions, and so on. Later, you pair the students and give them a few basic questions to discuss. For this activity, you might choose to pair a more advanced student with a less advanced one. Is this starting to make sense?

Some will need life vests when initially being introduced to deeper waters. That's okay. Once they become more comfortable and adept in their skills, the life vest may be removed in favor of having you swim right next to them for a while. Soon your presence won't be needed. That's effective teaching. Eventually, each will be able to swim. Some will be more advanced than others—as is the case with any skill. And how you "get them to the final goal" will look different for some. The bottom line is that you get them there, taking them from where they are and moving them forward.

Can you see how you can bring this general concept into anything you teach?

TRY THIS

The following are a few ways to meet the needs of varied learners:

- Vary your activities.

- Give students a choice. Sometimes you can give students options to pick from when learning a new skill.

- Give students a voice. Listen to them and observe them. Learn about how they learn best.

- Include visual, auditory, oral, and kinesthetic types of activities in your lessons.

- Often you will teach in small groups, but keep those groups fluid—meaning don't simply divide your class into high, average, and low. Though sometimes your groups will be divided by ability, other times they will be divided based on interests, ability differences as opposed to ability similarities, experiences, and so forth. No student should be stuck in the same group each time.

- Remember that no student can learn anything at anyone's level but his own. So find out where each student is and work from there.

- Begin with small steps. If you're not accustomed to teaching this way, do what beginning swimmers do: get your feet wet first. Maybe start by adding one new type of activity into your teaching each day. If that's too much for you, start with one a week. But start.

- Maximize the use of technology. There are so many opportunities now for students to work at computer stations on specific skills, moving at their own pace while we assist other students.

- For each lesson, prepare materials to accommodate students of varying levels. If one student is advanced, be prepared to have something available to take him even further while you work with the others who are not as advanced yet. This is not to suggest that you let the advanced students teach themselves. They still need your guidance, too. But many times, they can handle more independent tasks than a student who needs to be taught the basic components of a particular skill.

- Ask for help and ideas from others.

DON'T FORGET

You are teaching your students to "swim" around in learning, thinking, and problem solving. How they get there will not look the same. But the end result should look quite similar. Yes, some students may go on to become competitive, award-winning swimmers. Others may simply enjoy a day at the pool on occasion. But if any of them ever fell into deep water, they could all make their way safely to the side of the pool. Mission accomplished.

42

YOUR STUDENTS DON'T STAY ON TASK FOR LONG PERIODS OF TIME

IF THIS HAPPENS

While watching television, do you change the channel often? Have you ever gotten agitated sitting in traffic, even when you're in no hurry to get to your destination? Have you ever found yourself daydreaming in the middle of a conversation, listening to another's story? Do you have trouble sitting for long periods of time? If you answered yes to any or all of those, it does not necessarily point to an attention disorder. You see, even adults without attention deficits have trouble paying attention for more than a few minutes at a time—unless there is some type of "movement" or "change" during the activity. Yet many adults expect students to sit and focus for lengthy periods of time. We see this often in the classroom.

We observed a teacher who was struggling to keep the attention of her students. She began the lesson with a lengthy explanation of the concept she was trying to teach. There was no interaction with the students. It sounded as though she was reading a script. Many students stopped paying attention after about two minutes. Next, she gave them an assignment—which she estimated (in her lesson plan) to last twenty minutes. Need we tell you how quickly the students were off task? During the first ten minutes, she was going from student to student, telling them to get busy, answering questions they had regarding the concept (remember that most had not paid attention to the teacher's explanation of the concept), and showing frustration. Finally, she said, "It seems that you need more explanation." She proceeded to repeat the original explanation of the concept—in the same way. She lost the students again, from the beginning. Then she tried to get them busy again—and, well, you can imagine how the rest of the lesson went.

During the conference following the lesson, the teacher said to us, "Did you notice how they don't pay attention? Did you hear how many times I had to redirect them?" And then she went into a soliloquy on the evils of today's world. Though we'll spare you of all the details, suffice it to say that she was so busy blaming society and social media and video games that she had forgotten to analyze her own teaching.

After three observations of this teacher, a clear pattern emerged:

- Explanations of concepts were long and boring.
- Activities—and we use this term loosely—did not contain much activity.
- Activities were too lengthy.
- Students were rarely actively engaged in learning.
- There was a lack of fun.
- The teacher appeared bored with her own lessons.
- There was an overuse of busy work.

The teacher was convinced that she was a victim of "today's students who grow up in today's world." She truly did not know that there were little things she could do that would make a big difference in the attention (and achievement) of her students.

TRY THIS

First, understand that it is rare for a student to be able to stay focused for any length of time, unless there is something to break up the activity and refocus the student. For instance, you may begin explaining a concept and break up the explanation with engaging questions. You may then have a student help you demonstrate something. You may lead an engaging discussion. You may tell a story to help students relate both to you and to the concept you are trying to teach. You may allow students to work together for an activity. You may have them conduct some quick online research about the topic.

Now, you might be asking, "What do you do when students have to work on a lengthy assignment, such as writing an article? That takes more than a few minutes." Yes, it does. So break up that activity. Stop every few minutes and ask them a question or provide them with something to think about. You're not interrupting their concentration. Rather, you're helping them to stay focused.

The key is that you keep things moving. The creators of video games figured this out a long time ago. That's why games are divided into levels, each with constant movement and increasing complexity. You start small, you grab their attention, you keep them engaged and challenged, you make it fun, and you let them go as far as they can go. That's it—that's just good teaching.

DON'T FORGET

Students' attention spans are short—very short. So teach in small bites, breaking up each activity and adding fun, excitement, motivating challenges, humor, and whatever else it takes. Yes, in many ways you have to be a "walking video game" if you're going to be an effective teacher. Grab them from the very beginning of the lesson (game) and keep them moving through each level, experiencing excitement, goal attainment, and success throughout. If they leave your classroom worn out but shocked that it's already time to go, you've succeeded.

43

YOUR STUDENTS DON'T PARTICIPATE IN CLASS DISCUSSIONS

IF THIS HAPPENS

Do all of your students participate eagerly and willingly in class discussions? Or do you struggle trying to coax them to participate? Do you have a few students who always participate, a few who sometimes participate, and a few who never participate? Shanna, a new teacher who faced these challenges, shared the following:

> I just can't get my students to participate in class discussions! It seems that the same few students participate all the time. Others won't even make eye contact when I ask a question. Some never volunteer answers or participate. They just sit there. I'm trying not to buy into the idea that kids today are lazy and simply don't care. So is it me? I'm worried that when I'm being observed, I'll be marked down for lack of student participation. I'm also concerned for the students because I realize that they need to be active participants in their own learning.

Shanna's challenge is a common one—and not just for new teachers. Observations of Shanna's instruction revealed that she was leading discussions and simply hoping that students would participate. Some did—the same few, every time—just as Shanna had noted. Others did not participate—at least not by raising their hands and volunteering answers.

There are a variety of reasons that students don't participate in class discussions. These include:

- They are afraid to give a wrong answer and risk embarrassment.
- They lack understanding of the topic being discussed.
- They do understand the topic of discussion, but are uncomfortable speaking in front of a group.
- They are bored with the discussion and have lost focus.

What Shanna didn't realize is that there is a variety of ways to actively engage students in class discussions, pulling them in and truly involving them. We shared a few of those with her, she tried them, and her problem was solved.

TRY THIS

We observed a teacher who has mastered the art of getting students to participate in class discussions. Here's how he does it: he holds a cup of Popsicle sticks with each student's name on one. As he discusses, he pairs students and tells them, "I'm going to ask a question, and I'll give you a few seconds to discuss your answer with your partner. Then I'll pull a stick and ask whoever's name I pull for the answer." (This way, he gives them a chance to think about their answer first and to discuss with someone else. This lessens the chance of embarrassing a student who does not know an answer or fully understand a concept.)

Another teacher shared that she puts her students into groups for class discussions and allows them to come up with group answers. Yet another technique involves having all students put their thumbs up. Discuss a concept and ask a question about it. Say, "If you agree, leave your thumbs up, and if you disagree, point your thumb down." This is a way to get all students participating and for the teacher to monitor basic understanding of concepts being discussed.

We've observed teachers who use an inflatable ball. The teacher asks a question and throws the ball to a student. That student has the choice to answer or say "pass" and throw it to another student.

Some teachers use apps on their handheld electronic devices that track student participation. This helps ensure that all participate several times throughout the day and no student is accidentally omitted from discussions. Correct and incorrect responses can also be tracked.

DON'T FORGET

When students are not participating in class discussions, try some of the techniques we've just shared. And remember that your own enthusiasm will help determine your students' level of enthusiasm. Be careful, of course, never to embarrass a student who does not fully understand a concept. Remember to reinforce the effort as opposed to only reinforcing the correctness of the answer. We want all students to be eager to participate in our discussions, and no one who feels intimidated will eagerly participate in anything. Also remember to keep discussions lively and interesting, with topics to which students can relate.

44

YOU'RE UNSURE ABOUT REWARDING YOUR STUDENTS

IF THIS HAPPENS

In one of our workshops we were approached by a frustrated teacher. "I've tried rewards, and they don't work," she reported. "The students have gotten so that they won't do anything unless there is some kind of reward attached. I should not have to reward my students for simply doing what they're supposed to be doing anyway."

Upon speaking more with this teacher, we learned that she used more bribery than anything else. When students were misbehaving or not paying attention, she would say things like, "Okay, anyone who gets busy right now will get a piece of candy at the end of class." She also used threats, bribery, and negative reinforcement quite often. When she anticipated that students might misbehave in a certain situation, she would resort to saying things like, "If you can behave well and participate while the principal is observing in this classroom tomorrow, we'll have a party on Friday." Okay, so what message did the students get? Didn't it seem like this could be used against the teacher? "We'll behave if you give us prizes, but that's the only way we'll behave." In other words, "No prize, no good behavior." The inappropriate use of rewards will backfire every time. Such was the case for this teacher. This teacher, however, admitted that *she* was motivated by rewards—rewards such as her paycheck, vacation days, Teacher Appreciation Week gifts, praise from her principal for a job well done, praise from her family for a delicious meal, and so on. When asked if she came to work only to receive a paycheck, she said, "No. I like to think that I'm making a difference, so that is part of my incentive to teach." When asked if she would still come to work if they stopped paying her, she said, "Of course not." She complimented her principal, saying, "She is very positive and always finds ways to show appreciation to her teachers." She then said, "Oh, I see where you're going with this. You're saying that students like to feel appreciated, too, even if they're doing what they're supposed to be doing anyway." Bingo!

It's nice to feel appreciated by others, and it's nice to be rewarded for a job well done. But rewards don't always have to consist of tangible objects. Sometimes rewards are more intangible—a word of thanks or praise, or simply the feeling of satisfaction coming from a certain accomplishment. Remember that it is human nature to work harder or behave better when an incentive of some type is attached. This applies to both children and adults. Rewards serve to motivate us to accomplish more or to behave better. There's nothing wrong with rewarding students, as long as you use those rewards judiciously and appropriately.

Be careful not to use rewards as a hammer. In other words, don't implement a reward system and then threaten students with it. This will devalue the purpose of rewards in the first place.

TRY THIS

Here are a few ways that successful teachers use rewards effectively with their students:

- Say thank you often, but don't say it unless you mean it, and unless the gratitude has been earned by the student. "Thank you for turning in your assignment on time." "Thanks for remaining quiet when I had to walk out into the hall for a minute."

- Use praise appropriately. "You did a very nice job of explaining your science project so that everyone could understand." "Your use of descriptive words in this paragraph made me feel like I could *taste* the food you were describing."

- Use occasional incentives. "Anyone who turns in all of their homework assignments this week will be rewarded with two free homework passes." "At the end of the month, anyone who has no negative marks for behavior will get to pick something from the treasure chest." "Each time you read a book from the list, you will get a check mark on the chart. When you have earned six check marks, you will receive a _____ (name the reward of your choosing)."

- Notice the good things that students do and point them out as often as possible. If you focus on the positives, you'll see more positives. The opposite it also true.

- Use stickers for students of all ages. Put a sticker on a paper or on the student's hand. Students love stickers, and stickers are inexpensive.

- Use learning games as rewards. "Since all of you have worked so hard today, I'm going to reward you with the _____ game." The truth is that the game is yet another learning activity, but the students see it as simply having fun.

The following are a few ideas for types of rewards:

- Edible treats
- Positive note that the teacher sends to parents
- Positive note that the teacher gives a student
- Thumbs up
- Verbal praise
- Coupon for extra points, free time, or to skip an activity
- Extra computer time
- Opportunity to run an errand for the teacher
- Stickers, pens and pencils, and inexpensive gifts
- Certificates of achievement
- Extra time to play a game
- Opportunity to work with a friend
- Expressions of appreciation

DON'T FORGET

All teachers want their students to behave well, work hard, and succeed. Effective teachers often use rewards—both tangible and intangible—to help them reach that goal. They don't, however, resort to bribery, and they don't put a negative spin on their incentive plans. In the classrooms of effective teachers, students appreciate the rewards, but don't expect them. There's always a nice balance of praise, appreciation, incentives, respect, positive relationships, and hard work.

We never get too old for gold stars and smiley faces.

45

WHEN BEING OBSERVED, YOU CALL ON STUDENTS WHO KNOW THE ANSWERS

IF THIS HAPPENS

Your administrator has told you that she will be observing you this week. She tells you what day and which class period she will be observing, so there will be no surprises. You have two days to prepare for this observation. You want to do your best, and you want your students to do their best. Of course, you do not mention the observation to the students, as you might be tempted to bribe them to behave and participate—which would be unethical.

Though you don't like to think of yourself as "putting on a show," you do want to demonstrate your best teaching. While preparing your lesson, you plan the typical types of activities that involve and engage your students. The lesson is ready, and so are you. Knock, knock. Your administrator arrives.

All is going well with your lesson. You teach and model a new skill, and now you want to lead a discussion. You ask a question, and you immediately call on a student who you know will have the correct answer. You do the same with the next question, and the next. You know you're doing it. You're calling only on the students who know the answers. This will make you look competent, right? Not necessarily.

Think about this: if the students already know the answers to whatever "new" content or skills you are teaching, then why are you teaching it? Isn't it a bit redundant and pointless to be teaching something they already know? Of course, you know that not all of your students know the answers, but the observer doesn't know that. Instead of appearing competent, you'll appear oblivious to your students' true needs—the very opposite of competent.

TRY THIS

Whether you're being observed or not, don't ever be afraid to call on students who may not know all the answers or may not be able to perform the new skills adeptly. This is your time to discern who understands and who doesn't. It's also a time to use your skills for dealing with incorrect answers—by letting students know it is acceptable to share an incorrect answer. You want your students to feel comfortable enough to take risks in your classroom and to be active participants, no matter what.

Once you get a good feel for who understands and who doesn't, you'll know who needs some remediation. Then, when you get the others busy, you can quickly and immediately provide some reteaching or remediation for those students. This, by the way, should earn you high marks on your evaluation.

DON'T FORGET

While being observed, it's human nature to be tempted to call on the students who know the answers. But remember: if they already know the answers, you're wasting their precious learning time. Effective teachers call on *all* students in order to determine understanding. If all understand, move on. If some understand and others don't, reteach those who don't. If no one understands, rethink how you just taught and reteach it differently.

46

A STUDENT ASKS A QUESTION AND YOU DO NOT KNOW THE ANSWER

IF THIS HAPPENS

You're very well prepared and are teaching your lesson. Students are interested and involved in the discussion. A student raises his hand and asks a question—a question regarding the subject matter you are discussing. You simply do not know the answer. Your mind races as you decide on how you will react.

You quickly come up with three options: (1) Say, "That's a great question, but I don't want to simply give the answer. I want to see who can find the answer first." And you get the class busy searching for the answer. Whoever finds the answer first gets extra points. (2) You say, "You must have read my mind. That's the question I was going to assign for homework tonight." The homework assignment tonight is for students to find the answer to that particular question. You'll obviously be doing that homework assignment, too. (3) You say, "Great question. I don't know the answer. Let's find the answer now." And the class does an immediate online search for the answer.

TRY THIS

Which option should you choose? You're afraid that option 3 will make you appear unintelligent or incompetent. That, however, is not true. Not only is it okay for students to find out that you're not perfect and you're not all-knowing, it's actually good for them to see how you handle yourself when you do not know an answer. Don't forget that the best lessons we can teach *any* student are how to find information, how to solve problems, and how to find answers to questions. Don't feed them the fish, but teach them to fish, and they'll be better equipped to meet the challenges of life.

The fact is that none of the three aforementioned options are wrong or bad. All three would lead to finding the answer. However, don't fall into a pattern of always choosing option 1 or 2 when a student asks a question to which you do not know the answer.

Remember that you are serving as a role model—and sometimes that involves modeling what to do if you make a mistake, what to say if you hurt someone's feelings, or, in this case, what to do when you don't know an answer. No one knows all the answers. Students should not see you as perfect—that's intimidating. If it's okay for you, the teacher, not to know everything, it makes the students feel better about the fact that *they* don't know everything.

DON'T FORGET

Students are always suspicious of teachers who are "never wrong." No one likes a know-it-all, even if that person is the teacher. In fact, when students view a teacher as a know-it-all, they try harder to stump the teacher. It becomes a fun game that they eventually win.

Yes, the teacher is supposed to know more than the students. But no teacher can possibly know it all. Admitting that you sometimes do not know an answer sets a positive example and provides an opportunity to teach them *what to do when you simply don't know.*

47

AFTER THE TEST, YOUR STUDENTS FORGET WHAT YOU HAVE TAUGHT

IF THIS HAPPENS

A teacher recently said to us, "I don't understand it. I work really hard at teaching something new to my students, and then they forget everything they've learned right after they take the test. If, next week, I were to give them the same test they took this week, most of them would fail!" We then asked her to tell us what she had taught and how she had taught it. It was a lesson about Abraham Lincoln.

The teacher had brought in famous quotes of Abraham Lincoln along with a historical timeline of his life. She had given the students vocabulary words on Monday. A brief lecture followed, and the students took notes. On Tuesday, the students read a chapter on Abraham Lincoln, then answered the questions at the end of the chapter. On Wednesday, they had gone over the questions and then read the chapter orally, round-robin style. A few more notes were given. The students were required to do online research to find answers to a few more questions about Abraham Lincoln on Thursday. There was a review, and the students were sent home to study for the test, which would be on Friday. So basically, the students had the job of memorizing notes and vocabulary for the test.

But where was the real-life application? Did the students get to know Abraham Lincoln? Did they delve into Lincoln as a person—analyzing his decisions, his policies, his core beliefs? Do they now realize how Lincoln's decisions affected life as they know it today? Did they compare him to themselves or people they know today? Did they predict how he might handle some of today's political issues? These are the kinds of activities that make learning stick. Memorizing notes does not constitute learning. And that's why the students were forgetting what they had "learned" once they took the test. They weren't actually learning anything.

This particular teacher was not lazy. She had actually worked really hard on her lesson plans. She admitted that she had never really thought about how she was teaching and why she was teaching that way. She said, "You know, that's just the way I was taught, so I did the same thing, never realizing that I wasn't engaging my students in the content and having them really learn as opposed to just covering the content and memorizing it." (See Topic 36: You Tend to Teach the Way You Were Taught.) This realization made her feel guilty about the way she had been teaching. We told her not to feel guilty. We're all continuously learning to be more effective in our teaching.

TRY THIS

If many of your students forget what they have learned as soon as they turn in their test papers, ask yourself the following:

- Am I helping my students relate the content I teach to their real lives?

- Am I allowing students to analyze, apply, and evaluate new material and use it to solve real-world problems?

- What is it that I want my students to learn and remember, beyond the test?

Ask yourself these three questions for every lesson you teach. These apply to all subjects at all grade levels. Students learn (and are more apt to remember) what they can relate to.

A few weeks after our first encounter with the aforementioned teacher, she said, "I've made a few simple changes to my teaching. The students are much more engaged now in my lessons. They're no longer forgetting what I've taught right after the test. And teaching for deeper understanding has made my lessons come alive. I can't believe the difference it has made."

DON'T FORGET

- Regardless of what you teach, you want students coming away from each lesson with learning that is relevant and that they can use in their lives. Students learn best when they can relate the content to their actual lives.

- Require your students to move beyond simple memorization of facts.

- If your students are forgetting what they have learned after they hand in their test papers, you may want to make a few simple changes to your teaching approach.

- Challenge your students to think critically about new information and concepts by engaging them in meaningful activities.

48

YOU LIKE A QUIET CLASSROOM

IF THIS HAPPENS

Mr. Control had been teaching for twenty-eight years. His hair was perfectly groomed, his attire was immaculate, his classroom was neat and tidy, and his students were well behaved. His classroom was referred to by the students as "the vacuum of silence." The only sounds emanating from his classroom were the drones of Mr. Control's voice as he lectured and gave instructions.

Across the hall was the classroom of Ms. Chaos. She taught the same grade level and same subjects as Mr. Control. But her classroom environment was anything but controlled. There was constant activity, constant noise, and chronic chaos. Ms. Chaos could often be overheard pleading with her students to settle down.

Both of these teachers were hard workers. Both genuinely cared for students. Both had the same goal in mind—student achievement. Yet both had some of the lowest test scores in the district.

Mr. Control just couldn't understand it. How could his students' test scores be as low as those of the chaotic classroom across the hall? Though it would be obvious to even the most casual of observers why Ms. Chaos's students had low test scores, it might not be quite as obvious why Mr. Control's students had low test scores.

Teachers like Mr. Control often fly under the radar. They don't struggle with discipline problems, so administrators rarely hear from them. When an administrator walks past the classroom, all seems well. In such a controlled environment, it seems that lots of learning must be taking place. But it isn't. *Remember that the one who is doing the doing is doing the learning.*

Gone are the days of the quiet classroom. In today's world, students need to be active learners and active problem solvers. And the only way to become active learners and active problem solvers is to become *active, engaged, and involved.*

TRY THIS

Many teachers are afraid of "noisy" classrooms. They're afraid that they might lose control if their students get too engaged and too involved. That, however, is simply a management issue. If your rules and procedures are in place (refer to all of Part Three: Classroom Management Challenges), keeping the noise to an acceptable level should not become an issue. Still, some teachers fear that if their administrator walks by and hears noise, he or she may think that no learning is taking place. Rest assured that no one—*no one*—is confused about the difference between "structured noise" and "chaos." The two do not sound even remotely similar.

Though most teachers will admit that a quiet classroom is a nice reprieve for the teacher, we all know that true learning rarely takes place in silence. The key lies in the structure of each activity. Let's say that you want to stage an active debate over a topic that's of particular interest to your students. As in any debate, there are conflicting viewpoints. Different "sides" emerge, and each side tries to convince the other of his or her viewpoints and beliefs. But there's always a moderator to keep all sides in check. That, of course, is you. The moderator spells out the rules of the debate prior to the actual debate. Throughout the debate, the moderator moderates. But both sides remain actively involved and engaged. They're champing at the bit to have their points heard and understood.

Isn't that what we want in the classroom? Though we're not suggesting constant "debates" going on in the classroom, we're using that analogy to show that the only way a debate would become chaotic is if the moderator didn't control it. We *want* our students to be champing at the bit to learn, express themselves, question, and solve problems. And again, that does not typically happen in silence.

Is there ever a time for classrooms to be quiet places? Sure. When students are involved in independent reading or independent writing activities, the classroom should be quiet. When students are taking a test, the classroom should be quiet. But the majority of the time, the classroom should hum with activity—structured activity. And, of course, the classroom is always a quiet place when the students are not there. That's your time to enjoy a quiet classroom.

DON'T FORGET

In order for true learning to take place, we should be continuously asking thought-provoking questions and involving our students in experiments, research, and problem-solving activities. Group work can be controlled or chaotic—it's up to the teacher. Discussions can be controlled or chaotic—it's up to the teacher. Learning games can be controlled or chaotic—it's up to the teacher.

49

YOU QUESTION WHETHER YOU SHOULD HAVE TO WRITE LESSON PLANS

IF THIS HAPPENS

You're feeling overwhelmed, overworked, underpaid, and underappreciated. Your lesson plans are due tomorrow, and the finish line is nowhere in sight. What can you do to ease your burden? Think, think.

The emotional part of your brain reminds you of the following: you've been teaching many years now. You've written thousands of lesson plans. You've taught the same subjects over and over. Why doesn't your principal just exempt you from having to write lesson plans? You could teach your lessons with your eyes closed, couldn't you? Yet your administrator still insists that you turn in detailed plans for every lesson you teach. Okay, so now you're wondering if you can just recycle last year's lesson plans. Will your administrator know if you turn in copies of the exact lessons you turned in last year? Probably not.

Enter the rational side of your brain, stage left (pun intended). You imagine a surgeon saying, "I don't need a surgical plan for your surgery. I've conducted this surgery thousands of times. You're just like everyone else, so I'll wing it with your procedure." Next you envision an airline pilot saying, "I don't need a flight plan. I've flown this route so many times I could get you to your destination with my eyes closed." And now you hear your wedding planner saying, "I know you hired me to plan your wedding, and I admit that I've never planned a perfect wedding, but I've planned some that were really great, so I'll just use one of those plans for your wedding." And finally you imagine your own child's teacher saying, "I'm tired, and I don't feel like writing the plans for the lessons I'm going to be teaching your child. I've done this many times, so I'm capable of winging it." Enough! You begin planning your lessons, realizing that failing to plan means planning to fail every time, regardless of how long you have been teaching. But you'd still like to make your planning more effortless and efficient.

TRY THIS

First, realize that there's nothing wrong with using some of last year's plans to help you with this year's plans. The optimal word, however, is "some." That's just good teaching—reusing what has proven successful and eliminating what has proven unsuccessful. (The problem is that some teachers tend to reuse some of their less effective material also, because they forgot to filter out what didn't work last year.) But last year is history, and it is quite possible that an activity that was relevant last year is no longer relevant today. Also, you are teaching *this* year's students, not last year's. Teach the students you have today in a way that accommodates their needs, as opposed to the needs of last year's students.

After you teach a lesson, keep what works and throw out what doesn't. But throw it out now. Don't just put the plan away, thinking, I'll remember next year to throw out this part. Chances are you won't. And be sure to include a few quick notes (it only takes a couple of minutes) on this year's plan in order to make it a better plan for next year. These notes might consist of ideas that came to you as you were teaching, suggestions made by students, and quick reminders to yourself of what you'll want to do with this lesson next year. Taking a few minutes to do this following each lesson will save you lots of time when planning next year. If you're struggling to come up with new ideas, read on to the next tip, Topic 50: You Need Creative Ideas.

And don't forget to plan for time to plan. Don't allow planning to become something you do whenever you find the time to do it, because you'll never "find" time to do it. Effective teachers schedule their planning time. They set aside a block of uninterrupted time each day specifically for planning. The fact is that an hour of uninterrupted planning time yields better results than several hours of interrupted planning time.

DON'T FORGET

When you're feeling like taking an easier route and slacking on your lesson plans, remember the following:

- "He who fails to plan is planning to fail" (Winston Churchill).

- By planning your "planning time" wisely, you can maximize your efficiency and minimize time spent planning.

- Try to set aside a specific time for planning each day—uninterrupted time spent planning in a quiet place.

- Organize this year's plans so that you can easily utilize some of these same plans next year. Again, the key word is *some*.

- Stay on top of your plans. Don't fall too far behind. You'll drown in overwhelm.

- Keep your plans current. An activity you used last year may not be relevant this year.

- Incorporate today's technology, not yesterday's, into your lessons.

- Keep what works, and throw out what doesn't.

- Remember that no one who wings it is effective, no matter how long he or she has been teaching.

- "If you don't have time to do it right, when will you have time to do it over?" (John Wooden).

50

YOU NEED CREATIVE IDEAS

IF THIS HAPPENS

You find yourself in a rut. You're bored with your own lessons. You have run out of ideas—and not just ideas for teaching content. You need ideas for motivating and inspiring students, you need ideas for motivating and inspiring yourself, you need ideas for organizing your classroom, you need ideas for communicating with parents, you need ideas for time management, you need ideas for dealing with challenging students. You need ideas, period.

Knowing you're in a rut and knowing how to get yourself out of that rut are two different things. (It has been said that the difference between a rut and a grave is the depth of the hole!) You can know that the drain in your sink is clogged, but that doesn't mean you know how to unclog it. Hopefully, we can help you to unclog your own personal "brain drain."

By collaborating, by not being afraid to ask others and share your own ideas—which may be old to you but would be new to others—you can also get creative ideas for how others manage their planning time, how others organize their classrooms, how others deal with disruptive students, how others motivate students, how others deal with parents, and so on.

TRY THIS

The following are ways that teachers can both become more creative and access the creative ideas of others:

- First, ask yourself, Am I truly open to new ideas and willing to take new risks? Far too many teachers are risk-averse. They fall into doing what they've always done because they know how to do it and they're comfortable (though often bored) with doing what they've always done. Thus, they lock themselves into safe mode and soon find themselves in a rut. Remind yourself often that if it doesn't feel fresh and exciting to *you*, there is little chance that it will feel fresh and exciting to your *students*.

- Ready yourself to step out of your comfort zone and try new things. Understand that trying new things can be scary. Then consider the alternative—not trying new things.

- Keep a notepad handy (either a paper pad or an electronic notepad on your phone or tablet) where you can jot down ideas as they come to you. Then bounce your ideas off of others. A little encouragement from a friend or coworker can go a long way.

- A quick online search can yield ideas for new, different, or better ways to teach the same old thing. Be specific in your search. For instance, you might search for "creative ideas for teaching area and perimeter." You'll find more ideas than you can possibly implement.

- Don't be too proud to ask your coworkers to share their ideas. Collaboration among educators fosters better teaching and learning. It nurtures a culture of sharing, creativity, and risk taking. It can also serve as a huge time-saver.

- Don't reinvent the wheel. If you're struggling to motivate a particular student and you know that another teacher down the hall has found ways to motivate that very same student, simply find out what that teacher does and do it.

- Utilize the tremendous potential of social networking to connect with educators around the world.

- Use your failures to forge a path to success. If a particular activity didn't work, analyze why it didn't, and do something different next time.

- Ask your students. Allow them to share ideas about how they like to learn, what they like to learn about, what motivates them, and so forth.

- There's nothing like activity to spice up a lesson. Plan for activities that actively engage your students. Turn an activity into a game, send students on a hunt for information, allow them to work together to solve problems, and so on.

- Observe fellow teachers whenever possible.

DON'T FORGET

When it comes to stepping out of your comfort zone and trying new things, don't jump into the deep end of the pool if you're just learning to swim. Get your feet wet first in the shallow end. Take it slowly. Try one new idea at a time, as opposed to throwing out your entire lesson plan and making it completely new. Baby steps eventually lead to full-blown walking.

PART FIVE

Professional Challenges

51

ANOTHER NEW PROGRAM COMES ALONG

IF THIS HAPPENS

Here we go again. Just when you had finally gotten accustomed to the latest, greatest new program designed to solve all of education's woes, having completed the training sessions, pored over the program's design, and finally gotten accustomed to making it "fit" into your own classroom with your own students and your own style of teaching, you hear the dreaded rumor: that program is passé, because there is something later and greater that will work even better. Really? What about all the money spent on the previous program for all of those materials and all of those training sessions? What about all the precious time you spent learning the techniques to implement the previous program? But sure enough, here it comes. And the pendulum swings yet again.

TRY THIS

What do effective teachers do when a new program comes along? They don't get bent out of shape. Though they don't always welcome the upcoming training sessions and the inevitable learning curve of any new program, they do welcome the possibility of learning something new that just might work. They're realistic enough to know that no new program is the panacea for all of their teaching challenges, but they're optimistic enough to embrace the new challenge. If, after rising to the challenge and giving the new program their all, they don't feel the program is worthwhile, they speak their mind and offer suggestions and possible solutions to their administrators. That's it. That's all they can do. They know that, they accept that, and they sleep well at night.

When asked about a new program currently being implemented in her school, a teacher recently said, "This, too, shall pass." We asked her what she meant. Her response held great wisdom:

> I've been teaching for twenty-five years and I have more certifications than the law allows. I've seen the pendulum swing back and forth. I've watched countless educators and researchers debate what's right and wrong with education, and I've witnessed more potential cures than diseases. Every time a new program or standardized test or curriculum comes along, I smile and say, "This, too, shall pass." Because it will. But I've learned over the years that none of these cures have killed me. In fact, they've all made me stronger. I've been a part of some promising programs and some ridiculously weak ones. Therefore I've learned a lot about what works and what doesn't. Had I been left to my own devices, I may have taught the same way for twenty-five years. Instead, I've continued to become better every one of those years. I used to complain with fellow teachers when faced with new trends, fads, programs, or philosophies about how best to teach students. But not anymore. Now, when a new program comes along, I actually welcome it, knowing that I will come out on the other end of it a better teacher. That, of course, will have a positive impact on my students. If you're going to be a teacher, you have to know that we're all learning and experimenting and growing together.

DON'T FORGET

When faced with the challenge of a new program, first, take a deep breath. Then remember the following:

- Teaching is like medicine. We are continually striving for new cures, new treatments, and better ways of servicing our patients (or students).

That's a good thing. We have to continue to experiment if we're ever going to move forward. Sometimes our experiments succeed and sometimes they don't. Accept that fact as a necessary part of the job. It's not going to change. The day we stop experimenting, we give up—on students and on ourselves.

- No one has ever become a less effective teacher due to the implementation of a new program. That's because programs are only as good or as bad as the people implementing them. So you have absolutely nothing to lose by trying something new and different.

- An effective teacher can take a not-so-good program and make it successful. An ineffective teacher can take a wonderful program and make it fail miserably. Give an excellent teacher an excellent program, and magic can happen.

- If your school has adopted a new program, give it your all. Whether it's a good program or a not-so-good program, it, too, shall pass. But *you* can be better regardless.

52

THE PERSON AWARDED "TEACHER OF THE YEAR" DOES NOT DESERVE IT

IF THIS HAPPENS

On every faculty there are excellent teachers, there are less-than-excellent teachers, and there are those who fall below the less-than-excellent bar. On your own faculty, you know who falls into each category. Everyone knows. So it would seem improbable that anyone outside of the "excellent" category could ever be considered for the coveted Teacher of the Year award, determined by the votes of teachers and administrators. But this year, it has happened. Ms. Doom, the teacher who barks at students, who complains about everything and everyone, and who serves as the head of the gossip committee has been named Teacher of the Year.

You are upset by this fact. You know she is not deserving of such a title. You believe that her "gossip groupies" joined forces to vote for one of their own, outsmarting (by outvoting) the many deserving teachers on the faculty. This is patently unfair. What can you do?

TRY THIS

First, realize that you did your part—you cast your vote for someone you felt was deserving of such an award. Second, realize that Ms. Doom won fair and square. That doesn't mean she deserves it, but the fact remains that she secured enough votes to win. In actuality, she won an election. And that election had an award attached to it.

If the election results have raised concern with enough teachers and/or administrators, the school might want to revisit the process for awarding the Teacher of the Year. That will be for next year, however.

So what is the best way you can handle yourself and your feelings about the fact that Ms. Doom is your school's Teacher of the Year? Handle yourself like a true professional. Congratulate Ms. Doom enthusiastically. You might even take a lesson from what one principal did when faced with a similar situation:

> Last year, we cast our votes (like we usually do) for the Teacher of the Year award. In the past, the recipients were always deserving of the award. But last year's results were a little shocking. Mr. Samuels won the award, but he did not deserve it. He's negative, he's resistant to change, and he's ineffective in the classroom. But I couldn't change the outcome. He had enough votes to win. We have many excellent teachers on the faculty, and, as it turns out, the remaining votes were spread among all of them. But even though I couldn't change the outcome, I thought of a way to make the best of things. Since Mr. Samuels was now Teacher of the Year, I decided we would treat him that way. At the awards ceremony, I congratulated him earnestly. I told him we would all be looking to learn from him and that I would be asking him to share some of his successes with the rest of the faculty. Though this might seem underhanded or sneaky, that was not my intention. My intention was to hold him to higher standards. After all, he was going to be representing our school as Teacher of the Year. I began having conversations with him about qualities of effective teachers—their attitudes, their techniques, their sense of commitment to the profession. He contributed to these conversations, often speaking with the voice of an effective teacher. I told him I would be observing him more often in order to learn from him. I even began sending

other teachers to observe him, allowing them to meet with Mr. Samuels beforehand so that he could explain what they would be witnessing during the observations. Long story short? Mr. Samuels began performing better, and his attitude improved drastically. High expectations accompanied a Teacher of the Year title, and he attempted to rise to the level of those expectations. Did he outshine my best teachers? No. But he did improve dramatically. For the sake of professionalism, I never revealed what I was doing to any of the other teachers, but I'm certain many of them figured it out on their own. I don't, however, think that Mr. Samuels had a clue. He was Teacher of the Year, and he tried to live up to it!

DON'T FORGET

As the old saying goes, "A person might not be as good as you tell him he is, but he'll try harder thereafter." Even, and especially, if the person awarded Teacher of the Year does not deserve the title, treat him as if he does. Congratulate him, and tell him you'd like to learn from him. Turn lemons into lemonade. Remind yourself that since he won this year, at least he'll be ineligible next year.

If you feel that the process for selecting a Teacher of the Year is not one that guarantees that the best person wins, work at coming up with a more reasonable process. In the meantime, instead of complaining and dwelling on this year's results, accept what is and make the most of it, as any true professional does.

53

YOUR PROFESSIONAL LIFE IS AFFECTING YOUR PERSONAL LIFE

IF THIS HAPPENS

Mariel was a third-grade teacher who loved teaching and loved her students. This year, however, she was feeling overwhelmed. Between trying to implement the district's new curriculum, trying to deal with a few students who posed an array of challenges, being put in charge of yet more committees, and just the everyday workload of teaching, she was left feeling frazzled, impatient, and exhausted. She found herself spending more hours at school than ever before.

When she got home each day, she found herself knee-deep in lesson planning and grading. Even her weekends were consumed with school work. When she wasn't physically working, she found herself worrying about certain students, bemoaning her workload, and lamenting her all-consuming job. Family time and activities were put on the back burner. She often found herself being short-tempered with and unavailable to her family. They pointed this out to her, which only served to make her defensive and resentful. "What do they expect of me? I'm only one person who can only do so much. Don't they realize how hard I work?" Yes, her family realized how hard she was working. She was working so hard, in fact, that they hardly saw her. When they did spend time with her, she was preoccupied and strung out. Her children began acting out in a desperate attempt for her attention, which only added to her stress level and her irritability. Her marriage, too, was on thin ice. That ice was about to break, swallowing Mariel and her family.

But what could she do? She had to learn the new curriculum; she had to plan her lessons; she had to grade her students' papers. True, but she also had to find some balance, and quickly.

TRY THIS

If you recognize that your professional life is spilling over negatively into your personal life, you may want to take inventory and do some simple rethinking and rearranging. You *can* have both a professional life and a personal life without neglecting either. Here's how:

- Recognize that you have to separate the two. This does not mean that you won't ever discuss your professional life at home or that you won't ever bring any paperwork home. That is unrealistic and, quite frankly, not possible. Just don't allow one to suffer at the hands of the other.

- Establish a schedule. For instance, set aside a certain amount of time each day to work on school-related issues. You might decide that you'll stay at school an hour after dismissal and you'll set aside thirty minutes after dinner to do paperwork at home. On the weekends, maybe you'll allow yourself an hour each day to do schoolwork.

- Share your schedule with your family so that they know in advance the times you will be devoting to schoolwork.

- Remember that your family comes first. Make sure they know that and that your actions show that.

- Take a close look at how you spend your time at school each day. Are you maximizing your time during planning period? If not, do so. Making efficient use of your time at work will free up more time at home for your family.

- Learn to let go. You have to make a special effort to learn to leave work behind, both physically and emotionally, and be present for your family, physically and emotionally.

- Learn to say no. If you find yourself overinvolved in committee work or other extracurricular school activities, you may have to say no to some of them. Speak with your administrator or other committee members and explain that you have spread yourself too thin and need to delegate some of your workload to others.

- At work, do what has to be done today and leave the rest for tomorrow and the next day. Don't neglect your duties, of course, but also don't attempt to be superhuman.

- Though some students challenge you, and others have stories that break your heart, try to give them your all at work and then leave those thoughts at work. You can't help your students by neglecting yourself or your family.

- Plan some time for *you*. If you overtax yourself, you'll soon be no good to anyone else. You've got to take care of yourself in order to help take care of others. You may want to set aside some time to exercise, engage in a hobby, or spend time with friends. All work and no play never turns out well.

DON'T FORGET

Though your job is important, your family comes first. With a little bit of effort, you can find a whole lot of balance. This way, you won't neglect either your personal life or your professional life.

At work, realize that you can only do so much. You are not superhuman. Do what you can today, and then let it go. Tomorrow will be here soon enough. The new curriculum isn't going away just yet, and it will await you tomorrow. Though there are certain job responsibilities you cannot neglect, there are others that don't have to be done immediately. Be good to yourself and treat yourself every day to some alone time and fun time. If this sounds selfish, it isn't. Allowing yourself time to relax and enjoy life outside of work (and occasionally away from family) will help to keep you physically and emotionally healthy. Your family deserves the best "you" you can be, and so do your students. By finding the right balance, everyone wins.

If you don't take care of you, *there's little chance you can take care of your students or your family.*

54

YOUR PERSONAL LIFE IS AFFECTING YOUR TEACHING

IF THIS HAPPENS

In the previous topic, we discussed the problem of allowing your professional life to spill over into your personal life. Now we'll focus on the opposite—allowing your personal life to spill over into your professional life.

Just as students deal with difficulties in their home lives, teachers do the same. If you're a person, you're going to have personal problems from time to time. Let's face it—there are days when you just do not want to come to school. Maybe you're going through a relationship breakup right now. Maybe you're dealing with the grief of losing a loved one; maybe you don't feel well physically today; maybe your child is sick and you've had to leave her with a sitter; maybe you had an argument with a family member before you left for work today; or maybe you're just having a rotten day.

When you're dealing with any of these issues, it's difficult to maintain a positive demeanor. It's much easier to be grumpy with your students, to teach with less enthusiasm than normal, or to take your bad moods out on your students and coworkers. It's also easy to give less effort to planning and teaching. After all, you're going through a rough time. People should understand that. They can't expect you to perform constantly at peak levels, can they?

Consider this. You're boarding an airplane. Your pilot's performance will determine whether or not you arrive at your destination safely. But your pilot is having a rotten day. He's going through a divorce and is involved in a custody battle for his children. On top of that, the FAA is changing rules and regulations yet again, and now he has to go through yet more training. He feels overworked and underappreciated. So is it now okay for him to perform on your flight at any level less than his best? Is it okay for him to take his foul mood out on the passengers? Of course not. It's just not an option for him to be anything less than competent and professional.

Any professional must act professionally, regardless of the fact that professionals are human beings. But how do you do it?

TRY THIS

The first thing to do is to recognize and acknowledge that your personal life is or may soon be affecting your professional life. If you don't know it's happening, you can't do anything about it. So take an honest look at what may be happening. If you're simply having one bad day, and you know you can't possibly give your students the quality care and instruction that they all deserve, the solution is simple: don't come to school on that day. Use your leave time for such a situation. If you're dealing with a painful situation in your personal life—a situation that will not be resolved within a day or two—then you're going to have to make a decision. Will you continue to commit to teaching, or will you be unable to fulfill your duties and responsibilities? No one can decide that but you. But if you do decide that yes, you will continue in your job as a teacher, then you'll have to acquire the skill of faking it. Smile through the pain of your personal problems while you are at work. Keep your focus on work while at work. Remind yourself that the students deserve your best, and that your personal problems are not their fault or responsibility.

We're not suggesting that you ignore your own personal needs, feelings, emotions, and struggles. We're simply reminding you that you cannot allow those to spill over onto your students.

DON'T FORGET

Remember that your personal life is just that—personal. It cannot affect your professional life. It's not okay to have a bad day at school just because you're going through a difficult time at home. Though it's not easy at times to act upbeat, positive, and enthusiastic, remind yourself that your students need and deserve your best every day.

55

YOU DON'T HAVE TIME FOR ALL THE AFTER-SCHOOL FUNCTIONS

IF THIS HAPPENS

You're on an extremely tight schedule with teaching, lesson planning, grading papers, and tending to your family life outside of your professional life. As it is, you can't seem to fit it all in. And yet there are all of these after-school functions—recitals, ball games, banquets, awards ceremonies, student meetings, various committee meetings, and meetings to plan all the meetings!

You want your students to know that you care—and you really would like to attend some of their functions, games, etc. You want to participate. You know that it's important for your students (and their parents) to see that you are interested in them as people, not merely as students in your classroom. You would also like to participate in several of the various committees that do good work for the school. But just how thin can one person spread himself?

Some teachers feel as though they don't want to show favoritism by attending some events and not others, so they simply don't attend any. Others go to the extreme and run themselves ragged trying to be at all of these events and participating in all of the committees. Neither is a smart choice. But rest assured that there is an answer . . . And it lies somewhere right in the middle.

TRY THIS

Here are a few simple tips for participating in after-school functions, still leaving plenty of time for your personal life outside of school:

- First, take a look at your schedule. Decide on an average amount of time, per week, that you could dedicate to attending after-school functions. Let's say it's two hours per week.

- Next, look at the week's activities. If there's a sporting event that will last two or three hours, you don't have to stay the entire time. You can "make an appearance" and stay for maybe 30 minutes. That still gives you some time to attend other functions during the week.

- Find out, from the students, what activities they're involved in. Let's say that two of your students are competing in a gymnastics competition this weekend. You have plans, and you know you won't be attending. Instead, ask them to take pictures of the event so that you can post them in your classroom and/or on your online class page next week. On Monday, ask them about the competition, and post the pictures! Your interest is really what counts more than your physical presence.

- If you can't attend the band concert, ask a student to record it for you. Listen to a few minutes of it in your spare time, and then tell them all how wonderful they sounded!

- Congratulate the students on their successes, and encourage them when they experience defeat. Set up a bulletin board or electronic photo frame and allow them to bring in pictures of their after-school events.

- Keep abreast of your students' extra-curricular activities and wish them well before each event. Ask them about the event afterward.

- Occasionally send a note home saying, "I heard Maria did an excellent job at her soccer game yesterday. I'm really proud of her." That kind of support goes a LONG way with both students and parents!

- Be realistic about how many after-school committees you can reasonably volunteer for. Do your part, yes. But don't overextend yourself.

DON'T FORGET

You're only one person, and you can only do so much before jeopardizing both your physical health and your mental health. Keep both intact by making smart decisions. Do as much as you can within reason. And remember that your "interest" in your students' lives and their extracurricular activities is what matters most. You can still be an active participant without always being physically present!

56

PLANNING PERIOD HAS BECOME GRIPING PERIOD

IF THIS HAPPENS

Ah, the planning period—a blessing or a curse? That depends on whom you ask. No one will argue that teachers don't need more time to plan. And one planning period does not provide enough time for any teacher to plan all of his lessons. True. But one is better than none, right? Again, that depends on whom you ask. We've encountered more than a few teachers who say that their planning period has actually become counterproductive because it has turned into a griping period for some.

A teacher shared the following:

I've begun to dread planning period, because no planning gets done at all. I thought the idea was great at first—a group of coworkers collaborating on their plans and sharing ideas. I actually thought it would help to lessen my workload. But boy, was I mistaken! What happens every day is that we all get together and complain about everything that is wrong with the school, the parents, the students, the principal, and you name it. Not only do we not get any planning done, but we sit around complaining about the fact that they ask us to do too much and don't give us any time to do it. Yet we're wasting an hour a day that could be spent planning for some of those things they're asking us to do. I'm thinking about skipping the "group planning period" from now on. It's bad enough to waste an hour a day, but when I realize that

I'm walking out feeling worse than I did when I entered the session, it makes me question why I'm going there in the first place!

First, realize that it's human nature to find comfort in the fact that you're not the only one who feels overworked or frustrated at times. And there's nothing wrong with occasionally venting your frustrations to a trusted friend, family member, or colleague. But every day for an hour is a bit excessive. You'll begin to buy into all the negative dialogue, and soon you'll be "one of them." (See Topic 18: Some of Your Coworkers Are Negative.)

TRY THIS

Here are a few simple tips for making the most of your planning time:

- Don't participate in any of the griping. Period. Attempt to refocus that group on its purpose—to collaborate and plan. If you're not comfortable doing that on your own, enlist the support of other coworkers who also want to turn what has become destructive into something truly productive. This can be done without offending others by saying something like, "Why don't we get the planning piece out of the way first, and then we can leave the last ten minutes for open discussion."

- If your planning period is still not productive, don't participate. If you're allowed the option of planning alone or in a group, go it alone. But if you are required to spend that block of time each day with your coworkers, start working at making it more productive.

- Many times there are a couple of other peers who feel exactly as you do. Work hard to find them.

- Remember that it's good to collaborate with others, and we're certainly not recommending that you isolate yourself from this practice. We are, however, suggesting that you become part of the solution by helping to make planning period efficient, effective, and productive.

- It's okay to enlist the support of an administrator if the griping group outnumbers the others. It's not disloyal or unprofessional if a group of you discuss with your administrator that you might need some help in reorganizing the planning period and reminding everyone of its true purpose. And it never hurts for an administrator to drop in on some of your planning sessions.

DON'T FORGET

Any amount of time you can find at school to plan your lessons gives you at least DOUBLE that amount of time at home to do other things. The reason we say "at least double" is because there are so many distractions at home. You can get at least twice as much done in an hour of uninterrupted time away from home as you can at home, where there are a thousand other things (and people) calling you and pulling you in various directions. Planning time at school is *golden*. Use it wisely, constructively, and productively.

57

YOU'RE ASKED TO TAKE ON ALL THE TROUBLED STUDENTS

IF THIS HAPPENS

A new student enrolls in your school—a student who is enrolling there because he's been expelled from his previous school. He has a file as tall as you and a reputation that precedes him. Legend has it that he can make any teacher cry, bemoaning the day he or she chose to teach. There are four teachers who teach at your grade level or in your subject area. So you have only a 25 percent chance of having this student land in your classroom, right? Mathematically, yes. But you know that realistically there is a 100 percent chance that you will be teaching him.

It never fails. Your principal always asks you to take on all the troubled or struggling students. Whether they're struggling behaviorally, socially, emotionally, or academically, they all seem to land in your classroom. You know without doubt that your principal will soon be knocking on your door with the news of your new student. Knock, knock.

Should you be upset? Is this fair?

TRY THIS

Remember that the best surgeons are asked to perform the toughest surgeries. The most highly skilled engineers are asked to take on the most complicated engineering projects. And there's a reason that when you have a plumbing emergency, the best plumbers are never available, because they're in such high demand. So it is with teachers. Each year the parents beg for their children to be in your classroom. And the administration loads your roster with the most challenging students. You're in high demand, and you know it.

Does that make it any easier on you? No, it does not. Don't you have a right to feel just a little overburdened? Yes, you do. Shouldn't the other teachers who teach the same subject at the same grade level have an equal amount of challenging students in their classroom? They would if you weren't so darned good. Your principal always says, "I hate to ask you to do this, but . . ." or "I knew if anyone could reach him, you could."

So what can you do? Actually, you can do two things:

1. Accept the challenge for what it is—a chance to positively affect the life of a troubled student.

2. If you truly are overwhelmed and overburdened, you do have a right to speak with your administrator about that and tell her exactly how you feel and why. It's okay to feel that you're at your max regarding the amount of challenges you can handle this year. Hopefully, your administrator will hear you out and understand that you're actually not superhuman. But if there's any more room in your life for one more struggling student, take him on. He needs you.

DON'T FORGET

You might want to remind yourself—often—of the following:

- You are assigned the most challenging students because you're skilled enough to handle them. Be proud of that skill.

- Someone—usually everyone—has recognized your talent. Feel good about that.

- The most challenging students need the very best teachers. You're changing lives. Be honored for that privilege.

- Don't beat yourself up if you truly cannot take on yet another high-maintenance student. When you're maxed out, let your administrator know about it. We would remind you to be professional when you speak with your administrator, but people like you always are.

58

YOU'RE AFRAID OF SOCIAL MEDIA

IF THIS HAPPENS

You've undoubtedly read the stories of teachers being reprimanded or fired for inappropriate use of social media. You've heard about teachers posting inappropriate pictures, content, and comments. You've read about teachers having inappropriate conversations with students on social websites. You've probably even learned of teachers posting unflattering comments about coworkers, students, parents, or administrators on various social media sites. The news is replete with such stories, and you may even know someone who has gotten himself into hot water via social networking.

A young teacher shared the following:

It's my first year of teaching, and I've already gotten myself into trouble. I thought I was being careful on my favorite social media site. I had my privacy settings arranged so that only my select friends could see what I was posting. Hey, I admit that I post almost every detail of my life for my friends to see. We all do it. I post what I eat, what I think, where I go, who I like, who I dislike, and basically everything I experience on a daily basis. I use off-color language sometimes, but it's only for my friends to see. What's wrong with that? Everyone does it. But one of my students has an older sister who is a friend of mine. He got onto her computer and was able to access all of my posts. He then shared those with other students in the class. And yes, I admit that I had posted a few comments about negative situations in some of my classes. I had even bad-mouthed a few teachers.

One of my students approached me and told me that some of the other students were looking at my posts. I was mortified! And now I'm afraid the word will spread and I will be in trouble. What can I do?

Regrettably, this has become an all-too-common scenario—teachers getting themselves into trouble via social media.

On the other side of that, you know of many teachers who use social media quite effectively. *Social media is not bad.* On the contrary, social media holds limitless possibilities for professional growth. The part that's bad is the inappropriate use of social media. There are numerous sites now dedicated strictly to education—where teachers set up class pages and communicate daily with other educators, students, and parents after school hours. Pictures, videos, and blogs are posted of students proudly displaying or discussing what they are working on, what they have accomplished, and what they think and feel about various subjects. They are able to communicate with students in other schools worldwide. Social networking has made a big world much smaller and more accessible. So don't fear social networking. Just approach it with caution and responsibility. A good rule to follow is this: don't post anything online that could be harmful to you, your students, or your job if it fell into the wrong hands.

TRY THIS

Here are a few points to consider when using social media in your personal life:

- Make careful use of privacy settings, and make every effort to keep your personal social networking activity separate from your professional social networking activity.

- Understand that privacy settings are not always foolproof, so be careful about what you post on social media sites.

- Do not willingly allow students to have access to any of your personal social networking sites.

- Remember that, as a teacher, you are a role model in the school and in the community. Act that way when dealing with people in person or through social networking.

Here are some tips for using social media appropriately in your professional life:

- Follow your school's policy on social networking—always.

- Use social networking to post and read education blogs, to connect with fellow educators, to help your students connect with other students, to communicate with students and parents, and any other ways that will enhance learning.

- Share your rules and regulations for student use of social media as it relates to the school and to your classroom. Though you can't regulate what students do on their personal social sites at home, you can and must be very clear on how they are and are not allowed to use social media in the classroom.

DON'T FORGET

- Don't make the mistake of thinking that anything posted on social media is completely private. That's not always the case, and it may not be the case at all.

- Don't post anything on social media that could get you in hot water if read by your boss, your coworkers, your students, or their parents.

- Don't post anything you would be ashamed for your students or parents to see.

- Don't avoid social networking in the classroom. Use it in a way that is professional and that enhances learning.

- Make sure the students are continually reminded of appropriate versus inappropriate use of social networking in the classroom.

- Be very careful to separate your professional from your personal social media use.

- Use social networking to augment your professional growth and collaborate with fellow educators.

59

YOU WANT TO BE MORE POSITIVE, BUT IT'S DIFFICULT

IF THIS HAPPENS

Sarah and Renita were two new teachers on campus. At separate times, they were approached by Ms. Gloom, the most negative teacher on the campus. She seized the opportunity to introduce herself to each and then proceeded to warn them of certain "bad" students who were on their class rosters. Sarah responded by saying, "Oh my. Why did they give those students to me?" Following the conversation, she shared her fears with her colleagues. Her day, and possibly her first year of teaching, had been ruined. She was a new teacher, after all. They should have been careful to avoid giving her such challenging students.

Renita had the same experience with Ms. Gloom. Her response, however, was quite different. When Ms. Doom warned her of certain "bad" students that would be in her class, she responded by saying, "Great. Those kinds of students are the reason I became a teacher. I'm going to work really hard at letting them know I care and helping them to make positive, responsible choices." Following the conversation, she shared with a colleague that she looked forward to helping students who had trouble helping themselves. She resolved to make those particular students her special project this year. She was a new teacher, and she was grateful for the opportunity to make a difference from her very first day of teaching.

Do you see what happened? Two people had the same experience. One chose to respond negatively and the other positively. Being positive is a choice. The situation with Ms. Doom was interpreted quite differently by the two people who experienced it. One saw it as a year-long sentence of misery, while the other saw it as an opportunity to make a difference.

If it sounds as though it's easy to maintain a positive attitude, it's not always. But being positive is a state of mind more so than it is a stroke of luck. Since we as educators serve as role models for impressionable young students, it is vitally important that we serve as *positive* role models. Students already have too many negative influences in their young lives. None of them can benefit from yet more negative influences.

The fact remains that in any school, there are both positive and negative people. (Yes, Ms. Doom teaches on every faculty.) And in any given classroom, some days will present more challenging situations than others. When you deal with these challenges, try to do so in the most positive way possible. Though we don't want to attempt to make our students believe that everything about life is positive, we *do* want to help them adopt overall positive, optimistic attitudes about learning and about life in general. The best way to do that, of course, is to model optimism. Even when something negative happens, an optimist will search for the lesson to be learned. A pessimist will feel victimized. We hope our students adopt the attitudes of optimists.

But let's face it: teaching can be difficult at times. Students can be difficult at times. Our coworkers can be difficult at times. All true. But will you approach your professional life with optimism or pessimism? It's truly up to you.

TRY THIS

Here are a few simple tips for maintaining an optimistic attitude at school:

- Smile. Even if your smile is a little forced, it will serve to brighten your mood and the moods of the people around you. If you don't believe that, you haven't tried it.

- Post positive quotes or sayings in your classroom.

- Don't allow negative coworkers to determine your mood.

- When you find yourself in the midst of negative coworkers, do one of the following: (1) try to put a positive spin on the conversation, (2) change the subject to one that is more positive, or (3) politely excuse yourself from the situation.

- When a student is struggling with something, and you see that he is becoming negative and frustrated, smile, tell him you're going to help him, and then help him. It's far easier to change a student's mood than it is to change an adult's.

- Be a role model of optimism for your students and your coworkers. Though there will be days when you have legitimate reasons to gripe, resist the temptation.

- Remember the old saying: actions speak louder than words. Students are watching you every day. And students prefer to be in the company of optimistic teachers, not pessimistic ones.

- Even when it's not appropriate to smile—like when you have to discipline a student who has behaved inappropriately—you can still act calmly and professionally as opposed to negatively and sarcastically. You can also speak to her about how to handle the situation more appropriately next time. At this point you can smile and say, "I'm counting on you to handle that situation differently next time."

DON'T FORGET

On any given day, you will be faced with a variety of people and a variety of situations. Though some of these situations will be out of your control, how you choose to react to them is most definitely *in* your control. When faced with negative coworkers, either attempt to put a positive spin on the conversation or politely walk away. Make an effort to surround yourself with the most positive people on the faculty. And in your classroom, remember to try to find the lesson in any and all challenging experiences and teach your students to do the same. Your mood each day will help set the tone of the class. Remind yourself every day that the students are counting on you to guide them and that you do possess the power and influence to change young lives. Students need more positive influences in their lives. So be an optimist and make a difference.

60

YOU CAN'T KEEP UP WITH EDUCATION'S BUZZWORDS AND JARGON

Education's buzzwords, I can't keep them straight

And some of the acronyms I cannot translate

IEPs, GEDs, accountability to promote AYPs

PLNs, CRTs, help me, someone help me please

Grouping, looping, KIPPing, and flipping

On all these terms, my tongue is tripping

Anecdotal evidence, relevance, and rigor

The glossary of terms grows bigger and bigger

Differentiation . . . gamification . . .

Intrinsic and extrinsic motivation

Need a little more?

Add the Common Core!

IF THIS HAPPENS

Does this poem ring true for you? From ESEA to NCLB to Race to the Top. Whole language, grouping, block scheduling, flexible scheduling, brain-based learning, site-based management, team teaching, balanced literacy, accelerated learning, corrective action, curriculum mapping, graphic organizers, higher-order thinking, inquiry-based, school choice, cyber schooling, criterion-referenced, norm-referenced, merit pay, multiple intelligences, chunking, school-to-work, participatory learning, academic freedom, alternative assessment, full inclusion, alignment-based reform, social networking, and on and on. Some of these you remember from way back. Many of those have morphed into some that you can relate to today. If you're a new teacher, you don't even recognize a few we've just mentioned.

Acronyms and buzzwords come and go. Some stay around longer than others. But it is truly impossible to keep up with every one of the latest and greatest fads and trends. Rest assured that you are not alone if you didn't even recognize some of the buzzwords above. Is it important to remain current in your teaching? Absolutely. But knowing all the buzzwords and being able to decode all of the acronyms alone won't necessarily keep your teaching current.

TRY THIS

The following are a few suggestions for remaining up-to-date with the latest trends in education:

- First, stay up-to-date on what is happening in your school. If your school is adopting a new program, it is important to find out all you can about it and receive any necessary training.

- Helpful online education sites are too numerous to list. But a few quick Internet searches will reveal what's happening in education today.

- Join a professional organization or two. Most organizations publish journals or provide online access to blogs, articles, research, and the like.

- If you don't recognize an acronym or a buzzword that is being used in conversation, simply ask about it. Don't feel unintelligent. No one can keep up with all of education's current jargon.

- Join other educators online, through social media, and in person to discuss and evaluate what's trending in education. But remember, just because it's trending doesn't guarantee that it's *good*.

DON'T FORGET

It's important to stay abreast of current research and trends in education, but it's not necessary to master all of the terminology. Sometimes everything old is new again, and the latest buzzword is simply a new word being used to describe an old technique. Other times what's new is truly new. But relax. If something new comes around that truly does enhance teaching and learning, you'll learn about it soon enough. Do your job and teach effectively. Things like brain-based research aren't going anywhere, because researchers will continue to study how the brain learns best. But the terminology may change when someone thinks of a new, clever, or more appropriate buzzword because education overdoes words that *buzz*.

A FINAL WORD

We hope that you have found within these pages useful ideas and suggestions that will help you more effectively deal with teaching's many challenges and obstacles. Even if you have implemented just a few of these ideas, your efforts will be rewarded in the successes of your students.

Remember always to keep student success as your driving force. By doing this, you will realize that though teaching is not an easy job, its rewards far outweigh its challenges. Almost anyone who has experienced any amount of success in life can point back to a teacher's influence. You, as teachers, are powerful, influential people. You touch lives—every day of every school year. Many people are *better* people because of you.

If you'd like to share your own ideas, successes, and challenges with us, we'd love to hear from you.

Annette:
E-mail: AnnetteLBreaux@yahoo.com
Twitter: @AnnetteBreaux

Todd:
E-mail: Todd.Whitaker@indstate.edu
Twitter: @ToddWhitaker

All poetry in this book is the original work of Annette Breaux.

INDEX

M

Management skills, 111–113; characteristics of classrooms lacking, 112; consistency, 113; establishing procedures for activities, 113; learning activities to pique student interest, 113; and professionalism, 113; rules/expectations, establishing, 112; securing the attention of your students, 113

Misbehavior with substitute teacher, 123–125; "substitute drill," 125

Missing supplies, 55–57

Misspellings, in test writing, 165

Motivation, 67–70; as cycle, 70; igniting, 69–70

N

Negative coworkers, 73–75; actions of, taking personally, 74; avoiding, 75; body language/tone, mirroring, 74; counteracting negativism, 75; dealing with, 74–75; enabling, 74; praising, 75

Negative evaluations, 93–95; improving areas of weakness, 95; inaccuracies, addressing, 95–96; meeting with principal about, 94, 96

Negative remarks of a coworker, 89–91

Neutrals, 59

New programs, 205–207; and moving forward, 206–207; and teacher effectiveness, 207; welcoming, 205–206

New teacher, befriending, 149

New test items, 164

Noisy classrooms, 191–193

Notepad, for jotting down ideas, 200

O

Off-topic discussions, 137–139

Optimistic attitude, maintaining, 237–240

Organization: allowing students to help with, 108–109; of classroom, explaining to students, 108; struggles with, 107–109; tips for organizing your classroom, 108–109; Today and Tomorrow box, 108–109

Out-of-the-classroom issues, 133–135

Outbursts, 63–66. *See also* Angry outbursts; behaviors associated with, 63–64; temper tantrums, 63

P

Parental lack of interest, 77–79; causes of, 77; class letter/group e-mail, 78; class website/social media account, 78; communicating with parents, 78–79; conferring with a parent, 78–79; positive communication, 78, 79; positive phone calls, 78; student note to parents, 78–79